W9-BUW-860

Date Due

NOV 21 '67			
			JUN 2004
			JUN 09 ANS'D
			JUL X X 2015

ESSAYS ON
THE GREEK ROMANCES

BY

ELIZABETH HAZELTON HAIGHT

KENNIKAT PRESS, INC./PORT WASHINGTON, N. Y.

ESSAYS ON THE GREEK ROMANCES

Copyright 1943 by Longmans, Green and Company.
This edition published in 1965 by Kennikat Press
by arrangement with the Estate of Elizabeth H. Haight

Library of Congress Catalog Card No: 65-18607

Manufactured in the United States of America

Indexed in the ESSAY AND GENERAL LITERATURE INDEX

To

BLANCHE FERRY HOOKER

IN HONOR AND FRIENDSHIP

The Publication

of this book was made possible

by the

J. LEVERETT MOORE RESEARCH FUND

IN CLASSICS

and the

LUCY MAYNARD SALMON FUND

FOR RESEARCH

established at Vassar College

in 1926

PREFACE

IF ALL the world loves a lover, as the old proverb says, then this my book should win wide fame. For these Greek Romances of the first to the fourth century of our era seem still to be singing the immemorial refrain from the old spring-time song of "The Vigil of Venus" :

> Cras amet qui numquam amavit,
> quique amavit cras amet.

> "Let those love now, who never lov'd before ;
> Let those who always lov'd, now love the more."

At a time when fiction is the most popular form of literature, these wonderful old Greek stories of love, adventure and worship are half forgotten and rarely read except by the scholar. Yet here, as in epic, lyric, elegy, drama, oratory and history, the Greeks were pioneers. In the second and third centuries they had created four different types of romance (of love, of adventure, the pastoral, the satiric) which were to have great influence on French, Italian and English fiction. The student of comparative literature, the student of the history of fiction cannot afford to neglect these pioneer Greek novels.

Their appeal, however, should be just as great for the general reader as for the scholar. For here are stories that mirror the life of the Mediterranean world in the Roman Empire with all its new excitements of travel, piracy, kidnapping, the new feminism, the new religious cults. And through all the different types of romance except the satiric the Love-God holds supreme sway over the hearts of men. So human, so vivacious are the love-stories that I offer to my readers Longus' assurance of profit in his introduction to his Pastoral Romance :

"I drew up these four books, an oblation to Love and to Pan and to the Nymphs, and a delightful possession even for all men. For this will cure him that is sick, and rouse him that is in dumps ; one that has loved, it will remember of it ; one that has not, it will instruct. For there was never any yet that wholly could escape love, and never shall there be any, never so long as beauty shall be, never so long as eyes can see. But help me that God to write the passions of others ; and while I write, keep me in my own right wits." [1]

My hope in writing on the Greek Romances is that I may lure readers back to them. My essays aim to be guide-posts pointing the way. I venture to suggest that along with my book readers should peruse at least four novels of different types for which good translations are available. These are *Chariton's Chaereas and Callirhoe* by Warren E. Blake (beautiful in English and format) and three volumes of *The Loeb Classical Library : Daphnis and Chloe by Longus,* Lucian's *True History* (in Lucian vol. I) and the Latin novel which combines the different Greek types into one great synthesis, Apuleius' *Metamorphoses.* If I can win new readers for these my favorites, my writing will be as successful as it has been happy !

It is a pleasure once again to express grateful thanks to publishers and authors who have allowed me to quote material. I am indebted to the Harvard University Press for its courtesy in allowing me to quote freely from volumes in *The Loeb Classical Library* ; to the Clarendon Press, Oxford for the use of material from R. M. Rattenbury, "Romance : the Greek Novel," in *New Chapters in the History*

---

[1] Translated by George Thornley, revised by J. M. Edmonds, in *Daphnis and Chloe by Longus* in *The Loeb Classical Library.*

of Greek Literature, Third Series, from F. A. Todd, *Some
Ancient Novels,* from J. S. Phillimore, "Greek Romances"
in *English Literature and the Classics,* and from *The
Works of Lucian of Samosata* translated by H. W. Fowler
and F. G. Fowler ; to Longmans, Green and Co., for the
use of a quotation from F. G. Allinson, *Lucian Satirist and
Artist* ; to the University of Michigan Press for the use of
Warren E. Blake's translation of Chariton ; to the Colum-
bia University Press for permission to quote from S. L.
Wolff's *The Greek Romances in Elizabethan Prose Fiction* ; and for generous permissions for quotations from
Professor M. Rostovtzeff and Professor B. E. Perry.

My writing has been greatly facilitated by the coopera-
tion of the staff of the Vassar Library, especially of Miss
Fanny Borden, Librarian, who has provided me with a
study in the Library, patiently borrowed many books from
other libraries for me and shown unfailing interest in my
work.   A constant stimulus to my writing has been the appreciation of my colleagues and students expressed in in-
vitations to read different chapters of this volume to the
Classical Journal Club and to the Classical Society.   Finally my profound gratitude is due to the donors of the
funds which made possible the publication of these Essays.

CONTENTS

xi

ESSAYS ON THE GREEK ROMANCES

I

THE GREEK ROMANCES AND THEIR RE-DATING

THE term "Greek Romances" is applied to long stories in Greek prose, written from the end of the first to the beginning of the fourth century before Christ and later imitated by Byzantine writers. It was one of these last, Nicetas Eugenianus, who prefixed to his own romance a prelude of verses which described their content :

> "Here read Drusilla's fate and Charicles' —
> Flight, wandering, captures, rescues, roaring seas,
> Robbers and prisons, pirates, hunger's grip ;
> Dungeons so deep that never sun could dip
> His rays at noon-day to their dark recess,
> Chained hands and feet ; and, greater heaviness,
> Pitiful partings.   Last the story tells
> Marriage, though late, and ends with wedding bells." [1]

The subjects listed in these lines are typical of nearly all the novels.   An author selected new names for his hero and heroine and portrayed the same quest for love and adventure.   The young pair always marvellously handsome fall desperately in love and plight their eternal fidelity in a sacred oath.   Soon they are separated by misadventure or the cruel will of Fortune and suffer alone every misfortune and temptation, but by superhuman effort and often

---

[1] By Stephen Gaselee, "Appendix on the Greek Novel," in *Daphnis and Chloe* in *The Loeb Classical Library*, New York, 1916, pp. 410-11.

1

by the aid of the gods, they at last emerge triumphant and chaste and fall in exultation into each other's arms.

It was just because of this similarity of pattern that it became the fashion for critics to belittle these melodramas, to emphasize their similarities, and to disregard their individual characteristics and enthralling style. Erwin Rohde's great critical study, *Der griechische Roman,* was perhaps the first to treat them with the serious consideration which they deserve. Now Rohde's theories have to be in large part rejected because of new discoveries in papyri which have necessitated the re-dating of the extant novels and adding to their study fragments of novels hitherto unknown which help establish new types and give a basis for a new critique.

My own discussion is to be concerned with the novels themselves, their individual characteristics, their literary qualities, viewed on the basis of their new dating. For this reason I shall spend little time on the famous theories of the origins of the Greek Romances and on their precursors. For my purpose of intensive, literary study it is enough to present these in outline.

In regard to the origins of the Greek Romances, two special theories must be mentioned since they have had more vogue than any others. These are the theories of Erwin Rohde and of Bruno Lavagnini. Erwin Rohde in *Der griechische Roman,* which first appeared in 1876, recognized two essential elements in the Greek Romances : stories of love and stories of travel. He studied the precursors of these two types. He finally affirmed that the synthesis of the two, the romance, is a direct product of the rhetorical schools of the Second Sophistry which flourished in Greece during the Empire. Rohde based his work on the extant romances and the summaries of Photius (Patriarch of Constantinople, 858–886) and believing that none of this material antedated the second century of our era, he constructed his theory that "Greek romance was a product of the *Zweite Sophistik,* and had no direct connection either with the short story as represented by the Milesian Tales or with any Greek or Alexandrian literary form." [2] W. Schmid in the third edition of Rohde (1914) summarized in an Appendix the new discoveries and theories after Rohde's death.

I omit a résumé of the work of Huet,[3] Dunlop,[4] Chassang [5] and of Chauvin,[6] all significant in their times, to present a theory which is now more striking. In 1921 Bruno Lavagnini in a learned monograph, *Le Origini del Romanzo Greco,* traced the development of the Greek romance from local legends of Magna Graecia, Greece proper, the Greek Islands and Asia Minor. He found support for his theory in the titles of many of them :

Ἐφεσιακά	by Xenophon of Ephesus,
Βαβυλωνιακά	by Xenophon of Antioch,
Αἰθιοπικά	by Heliodorus,
Κυπριακά	by Xenophon of Cyprus,
Ῥοδιακά, Κωακά, Θασιακά by	

a Philippus of Amphipolis, which Suidas mentioned. In his study he took into account the novelle or short stories which Rohde believed had no influence on the novel, and studied the Μιλησιακά, the short *Love Romances* of Parthenius, the fragment of the *Aitia* of Callimachus, *Acontius and Cydippe.* He showed that Rohde had entirely neglected the important influence of the novella in the Greek romance and had been mistaken in his insistence on the

---

2 R. M. Rattenbury in *New Chapters in the History of Greek Literature, Third Series,* Oxford, 1933, p. 211.

3 P. D. Huet, *Traité de l'origine des Romans,* 1671.

4 J. Dunlop, *The History of Fiction,* Edinburgh, 1816.

5 A. Chassang, *Histoire du roman . . . dans l'antiquité grecque et latine,* Paris, 1862.

6 V. Chauvin, *Les romanciérs grecs et latins,* 1864.

fundamentally different character of the two. Rohde claimed that the novella was realistic, the romance idealistic and hence declared that any derivation of the romance from the novella was impossible. Lavagnini recognized other influences in the development of the romance, especially those of satire and of the new comedy, but he maintained that an essential feature was the historical. He admitted that in the use of his local legends the events are projected into an ideal and remote past.

The tendency in the new criticism of the Greek Romances, notably in the work of Aristide Calderini,[7] is not to seek for any one main source for their "origins," but rather to consider all possible precursors in the field of fiction who directly or indirectly influenced them. Their name is legion and they appear in the fields of both poetry and prose. For from the earliest times of Greek literature the art of narration was in use. Epics presented narratives of war in the Iliad, of adventure in the Odyssey, of love in Apollonius Rhodius. Drama produced narrative speeches particularly in tragedy in the role of the messenger. Elegiac poetry developed subjective-erotic stories, based on myths, or history, or real life, and written in lyric mood in narratives or letters. Idyls finally portrayed against a pastoral setting the outdoor loves of shepherds.

In prose, there are full-grown novelettes combining love and adventure embedded in the Greek historians : Herodotus' story of Candaules' wife,[8] the story of Rhampsinitus' treasure,[9] the story of the love of Xerxes,[10] the story of Abradatas of Susa and Panthea in Xenophon's *Education of Cyrus* which Whibley calls "the first love-

---

[7] *Caritone di Afrodisia, Le Avventure di Cherea e Calliroe, romanzo tradotto da Aristide Calderini,* Torino, 1913.

[8] Her. I. 8-12.
[9] Her. II. 121.
[10] Her. IX. 108-13.

story in European prose." [11]   Short stories or novelle in prose are known from the accounts of the Milesian Tales and from Parthenius' miniature *Love Romances*.   The Μιλησιακά were written in the second century B.C., by Aristides of Miletus and a collection of them was translated into Latin by Cornelius Sisenna who died 57 B.C.   Their character was definite : they were erotic stories of a lascivious type.   Their philosophy of life was that all men — and women — are sinners, and this belief was embodied in episodes from every-day life.   Their amorality was such that the Parthian Surena was horrified when in the Parthian War of 53 B.C., a copy of the Milesian Tales was found in the pack of a Roman officer.   Other short local tales, for example those of Sybaris and of Ephesus, shared these characteristics of realism, irony and disillusion.

Parthenius of Nicaea wrote a collection of short *Love Romances* of a very different type.   This Greek elegiac poet of the Augustan Age wrote his *Love Romances* in Greek prose as a storehouse for his friend, Cornelius Gallus, to draw upon for material for epic or elegiac verse ; and for this reason he put them forth in the briefest and simplest form possible.   Most of them are unfamiliar stories even when they are about well-known mythological characters.   In many the love tales are set against a background of war.   Short as they are, both their subject matter and style are significant for the development of Greek prose fiction.

Moreover, the work of the rhetorical schools must be considered among the forerunners of the novel, both in Greek and Latin.   Although we know now that the Greek Romances were being written before the time of the New or Second Sophistry which Rohde postulated to be their

[11] L. Whibley, *A Companion to Greek Studies*, Cambridge, 1916, p. 155.   For a discussion of these stories and the novelle see E. H. Haight, *Essays on Ancient Fiction*, New York, 1936.

origin, still in the Greek Romances as well as in the *Satyricon* and in Apuleius' *Metamorphoses,* there are many illustrations of the influence of the practice cases of the rhetorical schools.   A study of the *Controversiae* in Seneca the Elder and in the pseudo-Quintilian, a study of *The Lives of the Sophists* by Philostratus demonstrates that in these school exercises where "oratory became a theatrical fiction" [12] lay many first drafts of a new literary genre, the romance.[13]

It is a pity that Erwin Rohde could not have lived to revise himself his great work on the Greek Romances in the light of the new discoveries about them.   No scholar has yet arisen equipped with his tremendous erudition and penetrating criticism to succeed him worthily.   Perhaps indeed the time has not yet come to write a new critical history of the Greek romance, for at any time added discoveries may demand still further revision of dates and consideration of types.   But at this stage it is essential to review the new discoveries and to try to estimate their significance.   This outline is based on three important summaries : the introduction by Aristide Calderini to his translation of Chariton ; [14] the "Appendix on the Greek Novel" by Stephen Gaselee in the edition of *Daphnis and Chloe* and Parthenius in *The Loeb Classical Library* ; [15] and the chapter on "Romance : the Greek Novel" by R. M. Rattenbury in *New Chapters in the History of Greek Literature, Third Series.*[16]

Most spectacular and important of the new discoveries was that of the fragments of the Ninus Romance, first

[12] Alfred   Croiset   and   Maurice Croiset, *An Abridged History of Greek Literature,* translated by G. F. Heffelbower, New York, 1904, p. 517.

[13] H. Bornecque, *Les Déclamations et les Déclamateurs d'après Sénèque le père,* Lille, 1902, p. 130.

[14] *Caritone di Afrodisia, Le Avventure di Cherea e Calliroe,* Aristide Calderini, Torino, 1913.

[15] New York, 1916.

[16] Oxford, 1933.

published in 1893. They were found on an Egyptian papyrus, on the back of which are written some accounts of A.D. 101. The writing of the romance is so clear and beautiful that it is dated by experts as belonging to the first century B.C. As Rattenbury says : "The Ninus Romance is therefore the only pre-Christian specimen of its kind ; it is indisputably two centuries earlier than the earliest of the completely extant romances (Charito), and probably as much earlier than any of the known fragments." [17] The remains consist of two separate fragments with parts of five columns on the first and of three on the second. Gaselee writes of the content : [18] "in the first (A) the hero, Ninus, and the heroine (unnamed), deeply in love with one another, approach each the other's mother and set forth their love, asking for a speedy marriage ; in the second (B) the young couple seem to be together at the beginning, but almost immediately Ninus is found leading an army of his Assyrians, with Greek and Carian allies, against the Armenian enemy."

Fragment A is short enough so that we can read Gaselee's translation of it : [19]

"Ninus and the maiden were both equally anxious for an immediate marriage. Neither of them dared to approach their own mothers — Thambe and Derceia, two sisters, the former Ninus' mother, the latter the mother of the girl — but preferred each to address themselves to the mother of the other : for each felt more confidence towards their aunts than towards their own parents. So Ninus spoke to Derceia : "Mother," said he, "with my oath kept true do I come into thy sight and to the embrace of my most sweet cousin. This let the gods know first of all — yes, they do know it, and I will prove it to you now as I speak. I have travelled over so many lands and been lord over so many nations, both those subdued by my own spear and those who, as the result of my father's might, serve and worship me, that I might have tasted of every enjoyment to satiety — and, had I done so, perhaps my pas-

[17] *Op. cit.*, pp. 212–13.   [19] *Op. cit.*, pp. 387–93.
[18] *Op. cit.*, p. 385.

sion for my cousin would have been less violent : but now that I have come back uncorrupted I am worsted by the god of love and by my age ; I am, as thou knowest, in my seventeenth year, and already a year ago have I been accounted as having come to man's estate.   Up to now I have been nought but a boy, a child : and if I had had no experience of the power of Aphrodite, I should have been happy in my firm strength.   But now that I have been taken prisoner — thy daughter's prisoner, in no shameful wise, but agreeably to the desires both of thee and her, how long must I bear refusal?

"That men of this age of mine are ripe for marriage, is clear enough : how many have kept themselves unspotted until their fifteenth year ?   But I am injured by a law, not a written law, but one sanctified by foolish custom, that among our people virgins generally marry at fifteen years.   Yet what sane man could deny that nature is the best law for unions such as this ?   Why, women of fourteen years can conceive, and some, I vow, even bear children at that age.   Then is not thy daughter to be wed ?   'Let us wait for two years,' you will say : let us be patient, mother, but will Fate wait ?   I am a mortal man and betrothed to a mortal maid : and I am subject not merely to the common fortunes of all men — diseases, I mean, and that Fate which often carries off those who stay quietly at home by their own fire-sides ; but sea-voyages are waiting for me, and wars after wars, and I am not the one to shew any lack of daring and to employ cowardice to afford me safety, but I am what you know I am, to avoid vulgar boasting.   Let the fact that I am a king, my strong desire, the unstable and incalculable future that awaits me, let all these hasten our union, let the fact that we are each of us only children be provided for and anticipated, so that if Fate wills us anything amiss, we may at least leave you some pledge of our affection. Perhaps you will call me shameless for speaking to you of this : but I should indeed have been shameless if I had privily approached the maiden, trying to snatch a secret enjoyment, and satisfying our common passion by the intermediaries of night or wine, or servants, or tutors : but there is nothing shameful in me speaking to thee, a mother, about thy daughter's marriage that has been so long the object of thy vows, and asking for what thou hast promised, and beseeching that the prayers both of our house and of the whole kingdom may not lack fulfilment beyond the present time."

So did he speak to the willing Derceia, and easily compelled her to come to terms on the matter :   and when she had for a while dissembled, she promised to act as his advocate.   Meanwhile although the maiden's passion was equally great, yet her speech with

Thambe was not equally ready and free ; she had ever lived within
the women's apartments, and could not so well speak for herself in a
fair shew of words : she asked for an audience — wept, and desired
to speak, but ceased as soon as she had begun.   As soon as she had
shewn that she was desirous of pleading, she would open her lips
and look up as if about to speak, but could finally utter nothing :
she heaved with broken sobs, her cheeks reddened in shame at what
she must say, and then as she tried to improvise a beginning, grew
pale again : and her fear was something between alarm and desire
and shame as she shrank from the avowal ; and then, as her affections got the mastery of her and her purpose failed, she kept sway-
ing with inward disturbance between her varying emotions.   But
Thambe wiped away her tears with her hands and bade her boldly
speak out whatever she wished to say.   But when she could not
succeed, and the maiden was still held back by her sorrow, "This,"
cried Thambe, "I like better than any words thou couldst utter.
Blame not my son at all : he has made no over-bold advance, and
he has not come back from his successes and his victories like a
warrior with any mad and insolent intention against thee : I trust
that thou hast not seen any such intention in his eyes.   Is the law
about the time of marriage too tardy for such a happy pair ?   Truly
my son is in all haste to wed : nor needest thou weep for this that
any will try to force thee at all" : and at the same time with a smile
she embraced and kissed her.   Yet not even then could the maiden
venture to speak, so great was her fear (*or,* her joy), but she rested
her beating heart against the other's bosom, and kissing her more
closely still seemed almost ready to speak freely of her desires
through her former tears and her present joy.   The two sisters
therefore met together, and Derceia spoke first.   "As to the actual
(marriage ?)," said she . . ."

In fragment B the seventeen-year-old warrior is found
marshalling his forces, "seventy thousand chosen Assyrian
foot and thirty thousand horse, and a hundred and fifty
elephants," and at the end beginning the advance at the
head of his cavalry :

And stretching out his hands as if (offering sacrifice ?),
"This," he cried, "is the foundation and crisis of my
hopes : from this day I shall begin some greater career,
or I shall fall from the power I now possess." [20]

[20] *Ibid.,* pp. 397-99.

In this Ninus Romance as we have it, the name of the heroine is not mentioned, but her mother's name is Derceia and that is a close variant of Derceto, the name of the divine mother of Semiramis in the usual legend. So although the type is different from that of the queen of Babylon, the character is probably hers. It seems evident that this early novelist was, then, building his romance around historical characters. Rattenbury points this out and also shows conclusively that the characteristics of all the other romances are indisputably present in this early fragmentary story : [21]

"The impetuous but honest Ninus reappears clearly enough in the Theagenes of Heliodorus, and the lovesick maiden of unassailable virtue and almost intolerable modesty might be the heroine of any Greek romance."

Ninus pledges his faith as later heroes take an oath. He like them is the toy of Eros or Aphrodite. In the extant romances,

"The characters, the treatment, and even the plots are almost stereotyped ; and yet one difference is observable — a tendency to abandon an ostensibly historical background in favour of a purely fictitious setting. The relative dates of the authors are by no means certain, but the fortunate discovery of papyrus fragments of Charito and Achilles Tatius supports the view, probable on other grounds, that Charito is to be considered the earliest, and Achilles Tatius the latest. It is therefore of interest to notice that Charito, though his hero and heroine are creatures of his imagination, introduces some historical characters and some historical events ; his main story is fictitious, but he seems to have been at pains to lend it a historical flavour. Heliodorus, somewhat later, presents a picture of a fairly definite historical period, but no more ; his characters are all fictitious and there is no historical authority for the sequence of events which he describes. Achilles Tatius degrades romance from the realm of princes to the level of the bourgeoisie. His story is frankly fictitious, and he evidently had no feeling that romance should be related to history."

[21] *Op. cit.*, pp. 219–23.

Rattenbury goes on to illustrate his theory of the change from the semi-historical to the purely fictitious romance by a study of the Alexander Romance and the new fragments of other stories. The pseudo-Callisthenes Alexander Romance in the oldest version extant is dated about A.D. 300. But papyrus fragments indicate that a large part of the material in it goes back to a time shortly after Alexander's death. From the evidence of our late pseudo-Callisthenes version which probably followed tradition it would seem that history was treated as fiction and little attention paid to the love-story of Roxane which could have furnished such a lively erotic interest. New fragments of other romances show other great rulers used as heroes.[22] One is the Egyptian prince, Sesonchosis, called by the Greeks Sesostris. Mythological characters too become protagonists in romances : Achilles and Polyxena ; the Egyptian Tefnut, daughter of Phre, the sun-god, who took her adventures in the shape of a cat wandering in the desert of Ethiopia. Other fragments run true to the general type of the Greek Romances in manifesting now this, now that characteristic.

The sum total of all the fragments discovered up to date gives convincing evidence of two important facts : first, the extant Greek Romances are only a small part of the output of this genre ; second, the dating of all the fragments places them between the end of the first and the beginning of the fourth century of our era. The Ninus Romance is the earliest fragment, Chariton's the earliest complete romance, that of Achilles Tatius the latest. On this framework a chronological list of the extant novels arranged on the basis of proved data and the probabilities of internal evidence and comparisons, shapes like this :

[22] *Op. cit.,* pp. 223–254.

THE GREEK ROMANCES

Date	Author	Title
I Century B.C.	Unknown	The Ninus Romance (frag.)
Before A.D. 150	Chariton of Aphrodisias	Chaereas and Callirhoe
II Century A.D.	Lucian of Samosata	A True History
		Lucius or Ass (an epitome of the lost *Metamorphoses*)
II–III Centuries A.D.	Xenophon of Ephesus	Ephesiaca, Habrocomes and Anthia
II–III Centuries A.D.	Heliodorus of Emesa	Aethiopica, Theagenes and Chariclea
II–III Centuries A.D.	Longus	Daphnis and Chloe
About A.D. 300	Achilles Tatius of Alexandria	Clitophon and Leucippe
Byzantine		
XII Century A.D.	Eustathius	Hysmine and Hysminias
XII Century A.D.	Nicetas Eugenianus	Charicles and Drusilla (verse)
XII Century A.D.	Theodorus Prodromus	Dosicles and Rhodanthe (verse)
XII Century A.D.	Constantine Manasses	Aristander and Callithea (verse)
Also known by translation or abstract		
II–III Centuries A.D.	Unknown	Apollonius of Tyre (Latin translation)
II–III Centuries A.D.	Iamblichus, a Syrian	Babyloniaca, Rhodanes and Sinonis (abstract in Photius)
II–III Centuries A.D.	Antonius Diogenes	The Wonderful Things beyond Thule (abstract in Photius)
Not before A.D. 300	pseudo-Callisthenes	Alexander Romance

It is to be observed that from internal evidence Xenophon of Ephesus probably came before Heliodorus. Longus is *sui generis,* and so stands apart from the typical
genre of the novels ; in fact is a unique specimen of another type, the pastoral romance.

The new discoveries from the papyri with the conse-
quent re-dating of all known material has given a strong
impetus to new study of Greek Romances ; new editions
of text with translation are being brought out by English,
French, Italian and American scholars.[23]   The introduc-
tions to some of these editions, especially those of Calderini
and Dalmeyda, are the first distinguished literary work in
the field since Rohde with the exception of Samuel Lee
Wolff's monograph on *The Greek Romances in Elizabethan Prose Fiction,* New York, 1912.

The time has now come for a literary study in English
which will make available foreign criticism and present
perhaps some new ideas.   I plan to discuss in successive
chapters Chariton, Xenophon of Ephesus, Heliodorus,
Achilles Tatius and Longus, and to suggest something of
their influence.   Then I shall take up the Λούκιος ἢ ὄνος attributed to Lucian and his *True History* and finally I shall
show the synthesis of the novel of adventure and the true
Greek romance of love in the great Latin novel, Apuleius'
Metamorphoses.

[23] See Notes.

II

CHARITON'S CHAEREAS AND CALLIRHOE

THERE are two reasons for beginning a perusal of the Greek Romances with Chariton's *Chaereas and Callirhoe*. It is "the earliest Greek romance of which the text has been completely preserved." It is "a lively tale of adventure in which a nobly born heroine is kidnapped across the sea from Syracuse to Asia Minor, where her beauty causes many complications and she is finally rescued by her dashing lover." I quote from Warren E. Blake whose publication of the Greek text and a literary translation of it are a monument to American scholarship.

The date of the manuscript of this novel has been proved to be not later than the middle of the second century A.D., by the recent discoveries of papyrus fragments of it.[1] Warren Blake comments on the significance of these discoveries : [2]

"In view of the complete absence in ancient literature of any certain allusion to Chariton, he was long supposed to be the latest of the authors of Greek romance, and was dated, purely by conjecture, about 500 A.D. But by a turn of fortune as truly remarkable as any attributed by Chariton himself to that fickle goddess,

[1] *Pap. Fayûm*, London, 1900, I (pp. 74 ff.) and *Pap. Oxyrh.* 1019 (vol. VII. 1910, pp. 143 ff.), both of the early III century, found in 1906 and 1910.

[2] Preface to *Chariton's Chaereas and Callirhoe*, Ann Arbor and London, 1939. Throughout this chapter

I use this translation of Chariton by Warren E. Blake and the Greek text edited by him, *Charitonis Aphrodisiensis, de Chaerea et Callirhoe amatoriarum narrationum libri octo*, Oxford, 1938.

14

three scraps of his book have been turned up in Egypt during the last forty years. One of these scraps was found in company with some business documents which date from about the end of the second century of our era. Inasmuch as the place of discovery was a small country town to which new works of literature would not likely penetrate immediately on publication, and since in any case an expensive book is almost sure to be preserved longer than day-by-day business papers, we seem quite justified in setting the date of publication back some twenty-five or even fifty years. Thus it is probable that this novel was written at least as early as the middle of the second century, only about one hundred years later than most of the books of the New Testament."

The identity of the author is made known by the first sentence : "I am Chariton of Aphrodisia, secretary to the advocate Athenagoras." Aphrodisia was a town in Caria in southern Asia Minor. Its locality helps little in expanding the autobiography of the author out of this one crisp sentence. But the romance itself reveals more of his personality. His fondness for court-room scenes and his elaborate descriptions of them are what we would expect from a secretary to a ῥήτωρ or advocate. His learning is evident from his many literary and mythological references. And occasionally he steps out of the role of the impersonal narrator into his own character and speaks in the first person to his reader. We will come to feel rather sure of his interests and tastes as we read his πάθος ἐρωτικόν.

Before proceeding to outline the plot of the eight books of this romance, it will be well to clarify the story by presenting a list of the characters.

The chief characters are :

Chaereas, the handsome young Greek hero, son of Ariston of Syracuse
Callirhoe, the beautiful young Greek heroine, daughter of Hermocrates, a famous general of Syracuse
Polycharmus, a young Greek, the devoted friend of Chaereas

Hermocrates, the general of Syracuse
Theron, a pirate
Dionysius, the governor of Miletus
Mithridates, satrap of Caria
Artaxerxes, king of the Persians
Statira, his wife, queen of the Persians
Pharnaces, the governor of Lydia and Ionia
Rhodogyne, the sister of Pharnaces, daughter of Zopyrus, wife of
    Megabyzus, a Persian beauty.

The minor characters of importance are :

Leonas, a slave-dealer of Miletus
Plangon, a female slave of Dionysius
Phocas, slave and overseer of Dionysius, husband of Plangon
Artaxates, the eunuch of Artaxerxes
Hyginus, a servant of Mithridates.

The list of characters reveals at once a connection of
Chariton's novel with the Ninus Romance because of the
use of historical characters. Hermocrates, the great general of Syracuse who defeated the Athenians in the naval
battle, 414 B.C., is the father of the heroine and is referred
to repeatedly with the greatest pride. Artaxerxes, the
king of the Persians, appears in person in courts and in
wars. Historical events too are mentioned as if to give
a background of reality : the contests between the Syracu-
sans and the Athenians ; the war between the Greeks and
the Persians ; the rebellion of Egypt against Persia ; the
merit of Cyrus the Great in organizing the army.

Against such a background of plausible reality, the plot
develops along three main lines of interest : love, adventure and religion. The story begins with the introduction of the radiant young hero and heroine of Syracuse
when they fall in love at first sight at a festival of Aphrodite. Almost immediately they are married, but their
ecstatic happiness is short, for Callirhoe's many other suitors, angry at her choice, plot revenge. They make her
husband jealous by false stories of a lover whom his bride

favors, and, by staging a surreptitious admission to his house of a lover of Callirhoe's maid, convince Chaereas that his wife is faithless. In passionate fury he dashes to his wife's room and when Callirhoe overjoyed at his unexpected return rushes to meet him, he kicks her with such violence in the middle of her body that she falls down, to all appearance dead. Chaereas is tried for murder and pleads for his own condemnation, but is acquitted against his will by the appeal of Hermocrates.

Callirhoe is now given a magnificent funeral and buried with much treasure. The heroine, however, who had only fainted, soon revives, but while she is bemoaning her sad fate, a band of pirates, led by Theron, breaks open the tomb, steals the treasure, kidnaps the girl, then sets sail with all speed for the east. At Miletus, Theron sells Callirhoe as a slave to Dionysius, a noble Ionian prince. He soon falls in love with his slave, but learning her story (except the fact that she was already married which Callirhoe omits) respects her tragic position and woos her with delicacy and consideration. Callirhoe, on finding that she is two months with child, decides to accept the advice of the maid Plangon and marry Dionysius to give her baby a father. Plangon assures Callirhoe that the child will be considered a premature seven months baby, and she secures from Dionysius a promise to bring up as his honored children any sons of the marriage. Book III tells how Chaereas found the tomb empty; how Theron was captured, forced to tell the truth by torture and crucified; how Chaereas and his bosom friend Polycharmus went on a warship to Miletus in search of Callirhoe but were captured and sold as slaves to Mithridates, satrap of Caria.

Now Mithridates too had fallen in love with Callirhoe on seeing her at Miletus. On returning to Caria he discovers the identity of his slave Chaereas just in time to save him from crucifixion because of an uprising of his fellow-slaves, and tells him that his wife is now married to Dionysius. Chaereas writes a letter to Callirhoe full of penitence and of love and Mithridates forwards it by Hyginus, his faithful slave, adding another letter of his own promising Chaereas and Callirhoe his aid. Unfortunately these letters fall into the hands of Dionysius himself and that noble prince, in his mad passion for his wife, conceals from her the news that Chaereas is alive and makes a plot for the protection of his own interests. He appeals to Pharnaces, governor of Lydia and Ionia, who is also in love with Callirhoe, to help a scheme he has made. Pharnaces thus prompted writes a letter to Artaxerxes, King of the Persians, accusing Mithridates of trying to corrupt Dionysius' wife. The great King then summons Mithridates to a trial for plotting adultery and sends also for Dionysius and Callirhoe.

The court scene is full of magnificence and surprises. Mithridates has no fear because in answer to the denunciations of Dionysius he is able to produce as a witness Chaereas who swears to his innocence and friendship. Mithridates is acquitted and departs. Then the King dismisses the court for five days before adjudging whose wife Callirhoe is to be since now she has two living husbands. Meanwhile he intrusts the lady for safe keeping to his wife, Statira. Dionysius is torn between the promptings of passion and reason. Chaereas is in despair at the possibility of losing Callirhoe again. And Artaxerxes, the King, like all the other great gentlemen in the story, falls madly in love with Callirhoe for her beauty.

The King's passion makes him postpone the court trial a month on the pretext of a dream which demanded sacrifice to the gods. His eunuch tries to persuade the heroine to do herself the honor of submitting to the King's embraces, but only horrifies and offends her purity. Now Fortune again takes a hand in separating once more Chaereas and Callirhoe, for a revolt of the Egyptians is announced, the King must be off to war, and as usual the queen and her suite go with him. Callirhoe accompanies the queen by royal orders.

Dionysius of course serves as one of the King's generals. He has a crafty piece of news conveyed to Chaereas that in reward for his faithful service the King had given him Callirhoe. Chaereas, believing this false story, and no longer caring to live, enlists with the faithful Polycharmus in the Egyptian army to fight against his rival. He is allowed to collect an army of three hundred Greeks in memory of Thermopylae and with them captures Tyre. News of this loss makes the Persian King so anxious that he decides not to travel with all his retinue, but to leave the women on the little island of Aradus. Chaereas who is proving a valiant warrior soon takes the island and discovers Callirhoe among his captives. Both faint on seeing each other but since joy never kills, they soon recover and reunited tell all and forgive all.

Word suddenly comes that the Persian King has defeated the Egyptians and their King is dead. Chaereas and his men decide to sail home to Syracuse, but first in response to the plea of Callirhoe Chaereas sends his prisoner, the queen Statira, back to the King because she had befriended Callirhoe in her woes. Callirhoe without the knowledge of Chaereas writes a beautiful and affectionate letter of farewell to Dionysius, intrusting to him the care of her son. (Dionysius still believes he is the boy's father!) The ship of Chaereas is driven by fair winds to Sicily where Hermocrates and the people of Syracuse receive the hero and heroine in amazement and joy. Chaereas tells the story of all their adventures and Callirhoe ends the tale with a prayer to Aphrodite : "I beg thee, never again part me from Chaereas, but grant us both a happy life, and death together."

With this simple outline of the plot before us let us study the way in which the story is told. Notable first of all are the shifting scenes, for the action moves rapidly from Syracuse, to Miletus, to Caria, to Babylon, to the sea, to Tyre, to the island of Aradus and then at last back to Syracuse after the full circle of adventures. The contrast between the free Greek city of Syracuse and the oriental kingdoms is constantly emphasized, but it is the love of adventure for adventure's sake that spices the narrative. The settings include, besides picturesque descriptions of localities, court-room scenes which are full of contrasts : the murder-trial of Chaereas in Syracuse and the trial of Theron also ; the arraignment of Mithridates for adultery before the Great King in Babylon. Pageantry of weddings and of religious ceremonies also enrich the plot.

The characters are painted in bold, rich colors. Hero and heroine are so beautiful that they can be compared only to great works of art : Chaereas resembles the pictures and statues of Achilles, Nireus, Hippolytus, Alcibiades. Callirhoe is now Aphrodite incarnate, now Artemis. Love is enflamed by their great beauty and enters through their eyes at their first sight of each other. Chaereas is proud and arrogant because of his looks and so passionate that he is unrestrained in his anger when he believes Callirhoe false. The kick which he gave his bride is a blot on his character which the reader finds harder to condone than Callirhoe did. She declares that cruel Fortune forced her husband to this act, for he never before had struck even a slave. He is also so mercurial that he repeatedly gives way to despair and is repeatedly saved from committing suicide by his devoted friend and companion, Polycharmus. He appears in more heroic guise as a warrior when he joins the Egyptians against Artaxerxes and Dionysius, resolved to die in battle, and wins a great naval victory. He is generous in sending the captive queen back to her lord. And he fulfills the ideals of romantic chivalry by declaring to Callirhoe at the end that she is the mistress of his soul.

Callirhoe like Helen had the gift of fatal beauty so that all men who saw her fell in love with her and she incurred for a time the jealousy of Aphrodite. But in spite of every temptation her spirit remained virginal and she was persuaded to marry Dionysius only to give a nominal father to her unborn child. She meets misfortune with natural tears, but with more fortitude than Chaereas shows. And she rules her anger even when the eunuch of King Artaxerxes makes insulting proposals to her by remembering that she had been well brought up and as a Greek taught self-control. She handles difficult situations with a woman's intuitive tact as when she writes a consoling farewell letter to Dionysius, without letting her husband have the pain of knowing of it and its tenderness. By it she secures Dionysius' care for the son he still believes his own. She wins from Chaereas with gentle tact a promise to send back the captives Statira and the beautiful Rhodogyne to the Persians. And in meek devotion at the end she essays to win even the goddess Aphrodite to complete reconciliation.

Polycharmus is a type more than an individual, for he is to Chaereas what Achates was to Aeneas, the faithful friend who accompanies him through all adventures. With boyish zeal, he hides from his parents in Syracuse his plan to go with Chaereas on his search for Callirhoe, but he appears on the stern of the ship as it sails in time to wave a farewell to his father and mother.   His chief function is to encourage Chaereas and prevent his suicide. At the end on their return to Syracuse he is rewarded by being given Chaereas' sister for a bride and a part of the spoils of war for a dowry.

Dionysius is a sympathetic and noble character ; indeed his sins are all for love.   He is in deep mourning for his dead wife when Callirhoe is purchased as a slave by his manager.   Although he believes that no person who is not free-born can be truly beautiful, he is overwhelmed with love at the first sight of Callirhoe.   With tactful sympathy he draws out her story and believes it.   He never forces his passion upon her, but woos her delicately through his maid-servant, Plangon, and is overjoyed when Callirhoe finally consents to legal marriage for the purpose of raising a family.   Even then in spite of his desire he delays the marriage that he may do Callirhoe the honor of a great wedding in the city.   His happiness ,is complete to his mind when after seven months a son is born.   So it is because of his sincere love that when he hears that a Syracusan warship has arrived to demand Callirhoe back, he commends his slave Phocas who out of loyalty to his master had persuaded barbarians to destroy the ship and its crew.   Dionysius' only anxiety is that since some of the men escaped, Chaereas may still be alive.   This last fact he conceals from Callirhoe and to comfort her for Chaereas' supposed death persuades her to erect a cenotaph to her first husband's memory.   Later when he receives the intercepted letter of Chaereas to Callirhoe, he faints with grief and fear, but coming to he believes the letter forged as part of a plot of Mithridates to win the favor of his bride, so he accuses Mithridates to the Great King. Summoned to Babylon to the trial he is in constant terror,

for "he looked on all men as his rivals" knowing the dev-
astating effects of Callirhoe's beauty.   When Chaereas is
produced alive in the trial, he argues valiantly for the re-
tention of his wife with some telling thrusts at Chaereas,
but finally when he has lost his love, he bears his grief
like a man, having remarkable self-control, treasuring Callirhoe's affectionate letter as true solace, and devoting
himself to her son.   Dionysius, as Callirhoe reminds him
once, is a Greek with a Greek education.

Among the orientals, resplendent princes appear often
only to be numbered among the disconsolate lovers of
Callirhoe and because of their passion to assist in further-
ing the complications of the plot.   Such are Mithridates
and Pharnaces.   More individualized portraits are painted
of King Artaxerxes and Queen Statira.   Oriental magnificence is the aura of the Great King's personality whether
he appears presiding in the court-room, or hunting in
Tyrian purple with golden dagger and elegant bow and
arrow on his caparisoned horse, or riding to war with his
great army and his retinue : his queen, her attendants, his
eunuchs, all their gold and silver and fine raiment.   Yet
through this rich setting appears a wise ruler who takes
counsel of his advisers in times of crises, listens judiciously
to evidence in the court-room, and in war follows the military traditions of Cyrus the Great.   But he has his human
side : is influenced by wine, loneliness and the dark, and
succumbs to Callirhoe's beauty though he is married to
a great and subtle queen.   Hoping to win the object of
his passion he is not above machinations with his eunuch
who acts as his go-between and with optimistic hope of
success even has Callirhoe taken along with the queen
when he goes to war.   Yet when Statira is restored to him
by Chaereas' magnanimity, he welcomes her warmly although her news that Callirhoe is with Chaereas is like

"a fresh blow upon an old wound." He appears most human after hearing Statira's story of all that happened, for he is filled with varied emotions : wrath at the capture of his dear ones, sorrow at the departure of Chaereas, and final gratitude that Chaereas had ended the possibility of his seeing Callirhoe. Out of his own conflict of emotions, he breaks gently to Dionysius the news of his loss of Callirhoe and calls him away from personal sorrow by giving him higher responsibility in the realm. Artaxerxes is really made to appear in the novel as the Great King.

Statira is no less the queen. She is delighted when her husband suddenly intrusts Callirhoe to her care, regarding his action as an honor and a sign of confidence. She encourages Callirhoe with tactful sympathy and secures needed rest for her, keeping away the curious ladies who hurry to the palace to call. After a few days Statira can not resist asking Callirhoe which husband she preferred, but her curiosity is not rewarded for Callirhoe only weeps. As time goes on Statira's jealousy is aroused because Callirhoe's beauty outshines her own and because she is fully aware of the significance of the King's more frequent visits to the women's quarters. So when Artaxerxes is preparing to start off for war, the queen does not ask what will become of Callirhoe because she does not wish to have to take her, but the King at the end demands her presence. Apparently Statira never betrayed her jealousy to Callirhoe, for after Chaereas took captive all the women in Aradus, Callirhoe has only praise for her kindness to relate to Chaereas and calls Statira her dearest friend. Her generous happiness in being able to return Statira's courtesy by sending her back to her husband wins from Statira a just encomium : "You have shown a noble nature, one that is worthy of your beauty. It was a happy sponsorship indeed which the King intrusted to me." Callirhoe on parting commends her child to the queen's care and secretly consigns to the queen her letter to Dionysius. Statira is still a subtle enough woman to enjoy telling the King at once on her return without her rival : "You have me as a gift from Callirhoe."

Set off against the Great King of the Persians is Hermocrates, the general of Syracuse who defeated the Athenians. His greatness as an admiral is matched by his leadership as a citizen. At the trial of Chaereas for the murder of Callirhoe it is Hermocrates whose generous plea in his daughter's name secures from the people a vote of acquittal. He listens to the wish of the people assembled when they urge him to marry his daughter to Chaereas. When Theron, the pirate, is captured and the crowd at Syracuse is milling about him, Hermocrates insists on a public trial for him in accordance with the laws and after the evidence is presented it is by a vote of the people that he is condemned. Then Hermocrates asks the people to vote to send a ship in search of his kidnapped daughter as a reward for his patriotic services. Callirhoe's pride centers in her father no less than in her Greek blood. Her reunion with her father at the end of the romance is almost as moving as her restoral to Chaereas. Hermocrates shines forth in untarnished glory as a patriotic admiral, a leader of thought in a democratic state, and a devoted father.

The minor parts are painted with less subtlety. Theron, the villain of the story, is a black-hearted pirate dominated only by gain and self-interest, ready to save his life at the expense of his fellow-sailors. Slaves are presented as vivaciously as they are in comedy. Plangon, the maid of Dionysius, is a shrewd, cunning opportunist, ready to serve her master's interests but not without kindness to the distraught Callirhoe in her plight of pregnancy.

Artaxates, the eunuch of Artaxerxes, is venal, wily, complaisant and low-minded. As the confidant of Artaxerxes he takes his cues from his master's words, and solicits his favor by an attempt to seduce Callirhoe's heart for him. As a eunuch, a slave and a barbarian (says Chariton) he could not conceive that Callirhoe would not yield to the wishes of the King. When he is unable to persuade her by flattery, he threatens her with the King's vengeance. And when her words betray her love for Chaereas, Artaxates can call her only a poor, foolish girl for preferring a slave to the Great King of the Persians.

The use of the crowd by Chariton is another link between his romance and drama, for it often fulfills the function assumed by the chorus in tragedy, that is, the part of the spectator who comments on the action and interprets it. It is the people of Syracuse in assembly that persuades Hermocrates to wed his daughter to Chaereas. The crowd votes the crucifixion of Theron and attends it. At Miletus the crowd joins in Dionysius' prayer to Aphrodite to protect Callirhoe and her son. The crowd at Babylon is struck dumb with amazement at the radiance of Callirhoe. And when the Great King is to decide whether Chaereas or Dionysius is to be her husband, all Babylon becomes a court-room as the people discuss the rival partners. At the end of the romance, all the harbor of Syracuse is filled with men to watch the ship come in, and when Chaereas and Callirhoe are revealed on it, the crowd bursts into tears. All rush to the theater and demand that there at once Chaereas tell them his adventures. "Tell us everything," they keep shouting. They groan at his misfortunes. They offer prayers for the future of his son. They shout assent to his proposal to make his three hundred valiant Greek soldiers fellow-citizens of

Syracuse. Indeed the crowd is constantly the background of the action of the romance.

Various mechanical devices used in the development of the plot show Chariton's art of narration. Conversation as any novel demands is constantly used. Soliloquies are introduced frequently : at some emotional crisis, Chariton, instead of describing the thoughts and feelings of his characters, has them burst into speech to themselves. Callirhoe on hearing of the supposed loss of Chaereas with the warship laments his death and the destruction of her father's gallant vessel. Later beside the Euphrates river when she can no longer see "the ocean which led back to Syracuse," she upbraids cruel Fortune for driving her farther and farther from home. Again, in horror at the proposals of the eunuch, she laments all her misfortunes and expresses her resolve to die as befits Hermocrates' daughter rather than become the mistress of the Great King. So too Dionysius on the return of Chaereas, after attempts at self-control, bursts forth with despair and jealousy into a lament over the imminent loss of his love. At the same time Chaereas, believing that Callirhoe loves Dionysius and will never return to him from the wealthy Ionian, utters a bitter lament before attempting to hang himself.

Letters also are an important means of developing the plot in the Greek Romances, especially in Chariton. He uses seven letters.[3] Chaereas' first letter to Callirhoe is an impassioned love-letter with an appeal for forgiveness and for an assurance that she still loves him. This is a crucial letter in the plot because it is sent by Bias of Priene to Dionysius himself who conceals it from Callirhoe. Bias

[3] IV. 4, 7-10 ; IV. 5, 8 ; IV. 6, 4 ; IV. 6, 8 (2 letters) ; VIII. 4, 2-3 ; VIII. 4, 5-6.

sends a brief business letter with it. Pharnaces, governor of Lydia, on the instigation of Dionysius writes a letter to Artaxerxes accusing Mithridates of trying to seduce Dionysius' wife. This letter is important for the plot, because it motivates the trial of Mithridates. The Great King on receiving it dispatches two laconic business letters to Pharnaces summoning Dionysius and to Mithridates calling him to trial. The other two letters do not affect the plot, but reveal the characters of the senders. These are the letters in Book VIII of Chaereas to Artaxerxes and of Callirhoe to Dionysius. Chaereas proudly sends back Statira unharmed as the gift of Callirhoe to the Great King. Callirhoe with a woman's intuition comforts Dionysius for her loss by gratitude for his protection, by assuring him that she is with him in spirit in the presence of her son whom she intrusts to his care. She begs him not to marry again, but to bring up the daughter of his first wife and her own son, eventually marry them to each other and send him to Syracuse to see his grandfather. She includes a message to Plangon and ends with an appeal to good Dionysius to remember his Callirhoe. It is hardly strange that Callirhoe concealed this masterpiece of epistolography from her jealous husband, Chaereas.

The taking of an oath is often an important feature of Greek Romances. In Chariton, Dionysius swears solemnly by the sea, by Aphrodite and by Eros that he will marry Callirhoe according to the Greek laws "for the begetting of children" and will bring up any child she bears.[4] Dreams too play their part in the plot. In a dream Dionysius sees an apparition of his dead wife as she looked on her wedding-day. His slave Leonas interprets the dream as prophetic of his coming happiness with the newly purchased slave, Callirhoe.[5] Callirhoe in her sleep sees

---

[4] III. 2.　　　　　　　[5] II. 1.

a phantom of Chaereas who says to her : "My wife, I intrust our son to you." This dream determines her to bring up her baby and so to marry Dionysius.[6] In Babylon when she is dreading having to appear in court, she has a dream of her happy wedding to Chaereas in Syracuse. The maid Plangon interprets the dream as a good omen for future happiness.[7] King Artaxerxes had a dream of gods demanding sacrifice so he proclaimed a festival of thirty days throughout Asia. This delayed his decision between Chaereas and Dionysius, hence was most important for the plot because wars arose before the court was held and in them Chaereas and Callirhoe came together.[8]

Apparent deaths are a common device of the Greek novelists and Chariton's plot turns on two, the supposed death of Callirhoe from Chaereas' blow and her subsequent burial ; the reported death of Chaereas on his warship. Concomitant with such deaths are the unexpected reappearances which add the element of surprise, so essential for the characters and the crowd.

Descriptive passages are few and brief in Chariton and are often worked out in a suggestive simile rather than in a conspicuous purple patch. Chaereas was as "radiant as a star. The flush of exercise bloomed on his glowing face like gold on silver." Callirhoe, recognizing her lover, became more stately and lovely than ever, as a flickering lamp again flares up when oil is poured in.[9] Public ceremonies are described at more length : the funeral procession of Callirhoe,[10] her wedding to Dionysius.[11] Space is given too to the description of Artaxerxes' hunt, that favorite ancient sport ; [12] to storm at sea ; [13] to war.[14] But

[6] II. 9.
[7] V. 5.
[8] VI. 2.
[9] I. 1.
[10] I. 6.
[11] III. 2.
[12] VI. 4.
[13] III. 3.
[14] VII. 4.

all these descriptions are concise in their picturesqueness.

Finally clarity in the narrative is secured by repeated résumés of the story either by the characters or by the author himself. Callirhoe tells her tragic tale to Dionysius with such sincerity that he believes it and honors her as a free-born woman.[15] Polycharmus relates his adventures with Chaereas to Mithridates and thereby saves his friend and himself from crucifixion.[16] Chaereas at the end unfolds the whole Odyssey of his wanderings to the populace in the theater of Syracuse.[17] At the beginning of Book V Chariton epitomizes all the preceding part of the novel and at the beginning of Book VIII he recapitulates the preceding book and reassures his audience about the final book.

"Furthermore, I think that this last book will be the most pleasant of all to my readers, and in fact will serve as an antidote to the tragic events of the former ones. No more piracy or slavery or court trials or battles or suicide or war or capture here, but true love and lawful marriage! And so I am going to tell you how the goddess brought the truth to light and revealed the unsuspecting lovers to each other."

The happy ending which Chariton here forecasts is an essential feature of a Greek romance. For in this type of literature in which Chariton is a pioneer, virtue must triumph. The ethics demands that the hero and heroine must be noble in character as well as in station and that therefore justice must be done to virtue. The hero we have seen must possess personal courage and military courage. He must be capable of emotional devotion, first of all to his lady, then to his friend, and always to his father. His faults are those of pride, arrogance and passion and his moments of brutality are condoned by his contemporaries on account of his passionate temperament.

[15] II. 5.
[16] IV. 3.
[17] VIII. 7, 8.

He can be generous to his foes.   He can show pity to the
unfortunate.   But his sympathies, even when the type is
embodied in as noble a character as Dionysius, are evoked
by the free-born in distress, rarely by slaves.   The virtues
of the heroine are first of all chastity, then loyal devotion
to parents, husband and child, pride of family, generosity
of spirit and sympathy.   She is capable of resolute decision and heroic action if her chastity is menaced or her
dear ones are in danger.   Standards different from our
own best ones appear in the general attitude towards slaves
as an inferior class and in the brutality manifested in the
hero's kick, in executions on the cross, in torture of witnesses.   Cleverness and deception are traits which are
prized more highly than we admit now.   The noblest
sentiments expressed are in behalf of liberty and patriotism.

Religion plays so important a part in the romance that
it demands a full treatment.   Chariton's novel is dominated by two cults : the worship of the abstract goddess
Fortune, the worship of the goddess of love, Aphrodite.
At the end of Book I Callirhoe, just after she has been
sold as a slave, in a soliloquy, upbraids cruel Fortune for
all her troubles, for the goddess made her lover her murderer, surrendered her to tomb-robbers and now has let
her be sold as a slave.   Again Callirhoe, when she finds
that she is pregnant, reproaches Fortune for letting her
bear a child to be a slave.   And on the banks of the Euphrates in another soliloquy Callirhoe again charges Fortune with all her miseries and blames her for taking "delight in persecuting one lone girl."   Mithridates tells
Chaereas : "The whims of Fortune have involved you in
this melancholy drama."   Queen Statira, when captured,
exclaims that Fortune has preserved her to see this day
of slavery.   And the author of the romance as well as

the characters repeatedly attributes to Fortune the strange and sad misadventures of his hero and heroine. Callirhoe, Chariton says, "was overcome by the stratagems of Fortune, against whom alone human reason has no power. She is a divinity who loves opposition, and there is nothing which may not be expected of her." Throughout the romance Fortune seems to be conceived not as blind chance, but as a baleful goddess, who takes delight in cruelty and torture.

In conflict with her machinations is the power of the goddess of love whom the young lovers worship. As clearly as in a Greek tragedy Aphrodite's influence is predominant throughout the romance. At the very beginning, Chaereas and Callirhoe see each other for the first time at a festival of the goddess and immediately fall in love. The end of the romance is the prayer of thanks which Callirhoe offers to Aphrodite in her temple at Syracuse. Callirhoe is so beautiful that over and over she seems Aphrodite incarnate, now to the slave-dealer, Leonas, now to Dionysius, now to the crowd at the time of her marriage to Dionysius, now in Babylon. Prayers for aid are constantly offered to the goddess by Callirhoe, by Chaereas, by Dionysius, by Artaxerxes, and these worshippers offer their petitions in her temples in Syracuse, in Miletus, in Babylon, in Aradus and in Cyprus. Her power is acknowledged ; her favor is asked. Chaereas discovers Callirhoe is alive by seeing a golden statue of her which Dionysius had dedicated in the temple of Aphrodite near Miletus. Chariton himself in his résumé at the beginning of Book VIII records the influence that Aphrodite had in his story. When Fortune was maneuvering to have Chaereas leave his wife behind at Aradus, all unaware of her presence, "this seemed outrageous to Aphrodite," says Chariton, "who, though she had previously been terribly angered at Chaereas' uncalled-for jealousy, whereby he had insolently rejected her kindness after receiving from her a gift more superlatively beautiful even than Paris' prize, was by now becoming reconciled with him. And since Chaereas had now nobly redeemed himself in the eyes of Love by his wanderings from west to east amid countless sufferings, Aphrodite felt pity for him, and, as she had in the beginning brought together this noble pair, so now, having harried them long over land and sea, she was willing once more to unite them."

The final consideration about Chariton must be the style of his work. And first of all the inquiry rises to our lips : how did the secretary of Athenagoras become so distinguished in the art of narration ? Homer, I am convinced, is the master from whom, as Dante from Vergil, he took his beautiful style. The romance is rich in literary allusions, but beyond all others Homer is quoted repeatedly (twenty-four times indeed) and with great effectiveness. Sometimes a mere transitional phrase is adopted :

"while the words were yet on his lips." [18]

In descriptions the brevity and simplicity of Homer are used with such nicety that the language often trails off naturally into the very words of the epic. In the thirty day festival at Babylon

"the sweet savor arose to heaven eddying amid the smoke." [19]

Men are pictured fighting and in their close array

"buckler pressed on buckler, helm on helm, and man on man.[20]

And as the conflict joined and Chaereas rushed against his enemies, he

"smote them right and left and there rose a hideous moaning." [21]

---

[18] VII. 1 = *Il.* X. 540.
[19] VI. 2 = *Il.* I. 317.
[20] VII. 4 = *Il.* XIII. 131.
[21] VII. 4 = *Il.* X. 483.

Artaxerxes in his court is compared to Zeus among the assembled gods.[22]   A phantom of Chaereas appears to Callirhoe resembling him

"in stature, and fair eyes, and voice, and the raiment of his body was the same."[23]

When Callirhoe came into the court-room in Babylon,

"she looked just as the divine poet says that Helen did, when she appeared to 'them that were with Priam and Panthöos and Thymoëtes . . . being elders of the people.'[24] At the sight of her, admiring silence fell, 'and each one uttered a prayer that he might be her bedfellow.' "[25]

Besides this use of Homeric phrases in descriptions, quotations are frequently introduced in conversations as if Chariton found only Homer's words expressive to convey the thought of one character to another.[26]   But far more important than such uses of Homeric phraseology is the intensification of emotional coloring by a quotation from Homer at a crisis of poignant feeling.   When Callirhoe's nurse calls her to get up for it is her wedding day,

"her knees and heart were unstrung,"

because she did not know whom she was to marry.[27]   When Chaereas is told that his wife is an adulteress,

"a black cloud of grief enwrapped him, and with both hands he took dark dust and poured it over his head and defiled his comely face."[28]

When Chaereas is determined to set sail in winter in search of his kidnapped bride, his mother begged him to take her with him and cried in Homer's words :

22 V. 4 = *Il.* IV. 1.
23 II. 9 = *Il.* XXIII. 66–67.
24 V. 5 = *Il.* III. 146.
25 V. 5 = *Odys.* I. 366. See also IV. 7 = *Odys.* XVII. 37 ; VI. 4 = *Odys.* VI. 102.

26 II. 3 = *Odys.* XVII. 485, 487 ; IV. 1 = *Il.* XXIII. 71 ; IV. 1 = *Odys.* XXIV. 83 ; VI. 4 = *Odys.* XV. 21 ; VII. 2 = *Il.* XXII. 304–5.
27 I. 1 = *Il.* XXI. 114.
28 I. 4 = *Il.* XVIII. 23–25.

"My child, have regard unto this bosom and pity me if ever I gave
thee consolation of my breast." [29]

When Dionysius suddenly learned at a banquet that Chaereas was alive from reading his letter to Callirhoe,

"his knees and his heart were unstrung." [30]

When Artaxerxes was smitten with love for Callirhoe, he
lay awake all night,

"now lying on his side, now on his back, now on his face." [31]

When Chaereas and Callirhoe had their ecstatic reunion
on Aradus,

"when they had had their fill of tears and story-telling, embracing
each other,
'they came gladly to the rites of their bed, as of old.' " [32]

Enough illustrations of Chariton's use of Homer have
been given to show the manner of it. Different explanations of Chariton's constant use have been advanced.
Schmid thinks it is an indication of the influence of the
Menippean satire with its mingling of prose and verse.
Jacob believes it due to Chariton's desire to make his
style poetic. Calderini is more understanding. He thinks
that Chariton, thoroughly familiar with Homer, quoted
him to express worthily some noble thought and that he
saw the peculiar emphasis which a quotation from Homer
could give to the expression of a sudden, violent emotion.
He also uses episodes from Homer (the appeal of Hecuba
from the wall to Hector,[33] the apparition of Patroclus before Achilles,[34] the Homeric τειχοσκοπία).[35] More than all,
his style is usually Homeric in its brevity and simplicity ;
and in his use of quotations, of scenes and of style he is
the first example of those relations between epic and ro-

29 III. 5 = *Il.* XXII. 82–83.
30 IV. 5 = *Il.* XXI. 114.
31 VI. 1 = *Il.* XXIV. 10–11.
32 VIII. 1 = *Odys.* XXIII. 296.

33 III. 5 = *Il.* XXII. 82–83.
34 II. 9 = *Il.* XXIII. 66–67.
35 V. 5 = *Il.* III. 146.

mance which became so important in the mediaeval literature of the west.[36]

Other literary influences are apparent. The Milesian
Tales may have suggested Miletus as the locality for the
love-story of Dionysius. The Ninus Romance is the pre-
cursor of the historical element which paints a background
of realism through the use of historical characters, notably
Hermocrates and Artaxerxes, and through allusions to
actual wars. Drama contributed the language of the stage
to the description of the action. And at one crisis when
Chaereas, who is believed dead, is produced by Mithridates
in court, Chariton explains :

"Who could worthily tell of the appearance of the court-
room then ? What dramatist ever produced so incredible
a situation on the stage ? Indeed, you might have thought
that you were in a theater, filled with a multitude of conflicting passions." [37] In another passage Mithridates says
Fortune has forced the lovers to enact a very sad tragedy.[38]
New comedy contributed types of characters (particularly
the slaves), spicy dialogue and at least two quotations.[39]
The influence of history and especially of Herodotus is apparent in the use of local history, in narratives of adventure, in depiction of the adulation of the eastern sover-
eign, in the reflection of the great struggle between the
west and the east. The influence of the rhetorical schools
is seen in the court scenes which in both their cases and
speeches are strangely like those of the *Controversiae* of
Seneca and the *Declamationes* of Quintilian.

All these different literary forces combined to produce
a style of narration in Chariton which is at the same time
simple and ingenuous, yet rhetorical. His startling ba-

---

[36] Aristide Calderini, *Caritone di
Afrodisia, Le avventure di Cherea e
Calliroe*, Torino, 1913, pp. 154–58.

[37] Calderini, *op. cit.*, pp. 159–60 ;
V. 8.
[38] IV. 4.
[39] Calderini, *op. cit.*, pp. 163–64.

roque effects are achieved by just this variation from simple concise epic narrative with strong Homeric coloring, to intense dramatic moments of high tragedy, to comic scenes of slaves' intrigues, to love passages which before had found expression only in poetry. Probably Chariton learned the effective use of parallelism, contrast and surprise from the schools of rhetoric, but he wields all his various tools with such success that he has carved out a new form of literature in his prose romance.

III

THE EPHESIACA *OR* HABROCOMES AND ANTHIA

BY XENOPHON OF EPHESUS

"LET me not to the marriage of true minds
Admit impediments.   Love is not love
Which alters when it alteration finds,
Or bends with the remover to remove :

· · ·

Love's not Time's Fool, though rosy lips and cheeks
Within his bending sickle's compass come ;
Love alters not with his brief hours and weeks,
But bears it out even to the edge of doom.
If this be error and upon me prov'd,
I never writ, nor no man ever lov'd."

Shakespeare's famous CXVI sonnet is the lyric *credo* of those who believe that love can triumph over adversity, old age and even death itself.   The lines just quoted are the quintessence of lyric romance.

Suppose now that the romantic novel or the modern cinema wishes to feature this same theme : "True love lasts."   How would either one convey the idea ?   I am going to show you by a concrete and melodramatic illustration.   Here is a script for it.[1]

A young Greek who has been seeking over the world his kidnapped bride has come to Sicily, his resources nearly

---

[1] Xenophon of Ephesus, *Ephesiaca*, V. 1.

gone.   An old fisherman Aegialeus gives him hospitality.
It is night.   The young man and the old man tell each
other their sad love stories.   The old man is now speaking :
   "I was a wealthy young Spartan and loved a Spartan
girl, Thelxinoe.   She returned my love and presently we
had, no one knowing it, our heart's desire.   But my dar-
ling's parents proposed to marry her to another Spartan.
So we fled secretly together and Sparta pronounced sentence of death on us both.   We managed to travel to
Sicily.   Here we lived in dire poverty, but in our happiness we forgot all else because we were together.   Soon
my dear died, but her body was not buried.   I have her
with me and I love her always and I am with her."   After
these words he led Habrocomes into an inner room and
showed him the mummy that had been Thelxinoe.   She
was old now, but she appeared beautiful to her husband.
"To her," said he, "I always talk as if she were alive.   I
sleep here with her ; I eat near her.   If I come back tired
from my fishing, the sight of her comforts me.   For I do
not see her as you do, my son.   I see her as she was in
Lacedemon, as she was when we fled.   I see the night of
our first love.   I see our flight together."
   The young Greek exclaims :

"O my own dearest love, shall I ever find you even dead ?   Here
to Aegialeus the body of Thelxinoe is the great comfort of his life.
Now I have learned that age sets no bounds to true love."

   This story of the second or third century A.D. might
seem too macabre to be possible if the *New York Times*
of Nov. 12, 1940 had not recorded such a case at Key West,
Florida.   Karl Tanzler van Cosel, aged X-ray technician,
had removed the body of Elena Hoyas Mesa from its crypt
and had kept it in his bed-room for seven years.   He said
he had hoped to restore it to life.   Perhaps Xenophon of

Ephesus who wrote this story of Aegialeus and his mummy had heard some such "true story" which he embodied in his novel. In any case, he has given us here an illustration of how the theme "true love is eternal" may be pictured in a realistic romance. Think how dramatic this scene would be in a movie : the small inner bed-room of the fisherman's hut suddenly lighted ; the old man getting his young friend to help him remove the front of the coffin, then looking rapturously at the mummy inside and reaffirming before it his life-long love. That is my illustration of the heart of a realistic Greek romance.

Almost nothing is known about Xenophon of Ephesus who wrote it. Suidas mentions his romance the *Ephesiaca* in ten books (instead of the present eight) and speaks also of a work he wrote on the city of Ephesus. Xenophon probably was a native of Ephesus, for he shows intimate acquaintance with many details of the cult of Artemis there. His date can be given only approximately, but considerable internal evidence helps us to place him. He imitates certain passages in Chariton, so he must be later than the second century A.D. Certain references are very important. He is later than Augustus, for he refers to the prefect of Egypt and of course there was none until after 30 B.C.[2] He mentions the Irenarch of Cilicia, and this official was not known before Hadrian.[3] He refers to the Artemision of Ephesus as if it were at the height of its glory and contemporary.[4] It was pillaged and burned by the Gauls in 263 and only in part rebuilt. But, as Dalmeyda points out,[5] these details give us only vague indications of the date. Until some fragment of papyrus which can be dated is discovered, we can place Xenophon

[2] III. 12 ; IV. 2.
[3] II. 13, G. Dalmeyda, *Xénophon d'Éphèse, Les Éphésiaques,* Paris, 1926, p. 33, n. 1.
[4] Dalmeyda, *op. cit.,* pp. xiii–xiv.
[5] Dalmeyda, *op. cit.,* pp. xii–xv, xxxviii–ix.

merely with some probability about the end of the second century of our era.

The novel itself is simple in language and brief in scope, but complicated in plot from many kaleidoscopic changes of scenes. There are so many exits and reentries of the characters that we lose track of them. The brevity of the narrative, the laconic expressions of emotion in it have made certain critics maintain the theory that it is only an epitome of a story, or a kind of scenario written as a preliminary sketch of a longer work. It seems to me possibly an intentionally short romance written briefly and simply by an author whose taste was akin to that of Chariton and who perhaps was intentionally showing a definite reaction against the verbosity of other novelists.

Partly because of the brevity of the romance a synopsis of the plot has to be long. So much is crowded into small space, so many rapid transitions from scene to scene are made, that a full sequential outline must be given before we can study the significance and color of the romance. Here then is the plot. The chief characters are :

Habrocomes of Ephesus, the handsome hero
Anthia of Ephesus, the beautiful heroine
Apsyrtos, a pirate chieftain
Manto, the daughter of Apsyrtos
Moeris, a Syrian, husband of Manto
Lampon, a goatherd, slave of Manto
Hippothoos, a brigand
Perilaos, a high police official of Cilicia
Eudoxos, a physician
Psammis, a rajah of India
Araxos, an old soldier in Egypt
Cyno, his wicked wife
Aegialeus, a Syracusan who kept a mummy
Polyidos, a captain in Egypt
Rhenaea, his jealous wife
A procurer of Taras
Leucon, a male slave of Habrocomes and Anthia
Rhode, a female slave, his wife

In Ephesus lived a lad named Habrocomes who was sixteen years old. The beauty of his person was matched by the nobility of his soul. He had one great fault, pride. And he scorned Eros as less handsome than himself and unable to control a man against his will. Eros enraged armed himself against this arrogant boy. It was the time of the festival of Artemis. At this festival it was the custom to select fiancés. There was a great procession of young men and women. Anthia, daughter of Megamedes and Evippe, led the girls, and she was garbed as Artemis. She was so beautiful that the crowd forgot handsome Habrocomes though a few exclaimed : "What a couple Habrocomes and Anthia would make !" Here was Eros' opportunity. After the procession broke up and all were attending the sacrifice in the temple, the two saw each other and were vanquished.

Day by day, night by night love dominated them until both were worn out by longing. Their parents not knowing what this strange malady was sent embassies to the oracle of Apollo at Claros. The god diagnosed their illnesses as the same, needing the same cure ; he foretold long suffering for both, dangerous travel by sea, kidnapping, imprisonment, death and burial, but he promised final salvation through the goddess Isis and happy days.

The parents of Habrocomes and Anthia, puzzled and grieved by the oracle, decided that at least they must use the remedy suggested by the god. So Habrocomes and Anthia were married, and they did not fear the future because of their present joy. As time went on, however, it seemed necessary to the happy pair and to their parents that they should fulfill the oracle by going on a journey. On the ensuing voyage both swore mighty oaths (Anthia by Artemis) to be faithful to each other always. Next they put in at Rhodes for rest. Habrocomes and Anthia hand in hand visited all the city and dedicated golden armor to the sun-god in his temple. Then they sailed to Egypt, but the ship was becalmed and one night Habrocomes had a frightful dream. A giantess clad in red appeared to him who set fire to the ship, destroyed all the sailors and saved only himself and Anthia. He awoke in terror and terror became reality. Phoenician pirates arriving in a great trireme boarded the ship and drove the sailors into the sea where they drowned. Then they fired the ship, but took captive Habrocomes and Anthia and bore them off to the country near Tyre. Corymbos, one of the pirates, became enamored of Habrocomes; his bosom companion fell in love with Anthia, but before they could accomplish their wicked designs on them, the chief of the pirate band Apsyrtos arrived and appropriating the handsome young pair as part of his booty took them to Tyre.

This was the beginning of worse troubles, for while Apsyrtos was away on business, his daughter Manto fell in love with Habrocomes and made advances to him through a slave and a letter. When he refused to satisfy her desires, for vengeance she accused him to her father of having tried to rape her. Apsyrtos had Habrocomes flogged, tortured and cast into prison. Anthia contriving a secret visit to her husband told him she had been given as a slave to Manto and must accompany her to Syria, where Manto's newly acquired husband Moeris lived. The two slaves of Habrocomes and Anthia, Leucon and Rhode, were sold into a distant land. Manto to disgrace Anthia as much as possible married her to one of her humblest slaves, Lampon, a goatherd. But Lampon pitying Anthia on hearing from her own lips her story respected her and never made her his actual wife. In Tyre Apsyrtos happened to find the love-letter which his daughter had written to Habrocomes. Learning from it his unjust treatment of Habrocomes he released him from prison, gave him his freedom, and made him steward of his house.

Meanwhile in Syria Anthia's fatal beauty had inflamed Manto's husband Moeris with a mad passion for her. He confided this to the goatherd Lampon begging for his aid. Lampon to save Anthia went secretly and told Manto her husband's designs. Manto in jealous fury ordered Lampon to kill the woman. In sorrow he told Anthia all and together they planned that instead of killing her he should sell her as a slave in some remote district. He managed to hide this transaction and saved her life by selling her to some Cilician merchants. But their ship was wrecked in a storm. A few (among them Anthia) came to land on a raft and after wandering all night in the woods were captured by the brigand Hippothoos.

Manto meanwhile wrote to her father a letter made up of truth and lies, saying that the slave Anthia had been so troublesome she had given the girl to a goatherd and afterwards when Moeris became enamored of the woman, she had sold both the goatherd and his wife in Syria. Habrocomes at once started out in search for Anthia and finding Lampon and learning the true story from him, he set forth for Cilicia.

There, however, Anthia had been in great danger. Hippothoos and his brigands were about to sacrifice her to Ares, but she was rescued by a high police official of the district, Perilaos, who captured all the brigands except Hippothoos. He took her to Tarsus and of course soon fell in love with her. He offered her honorable marriage, wealth, children and she fearing his violent passion forced herself to consent but asked for a month's delay.

Now Habrocomes riding through Cilicia on his quest

met by chance Hippothoos who begged to be allowed to travel with him. They went into Cappadocia and there dining together told each other their life histories, Hippothoos his love of a beautiful lad and the loss of him, Habrocomes his love for the beautiful Anthia and his loss of her. The description of Anthia made Hippothoos relate his capture of a fair maiden and her rescue. Habrocomes, convinced that the girl was Anthia, persuaded Hippothoos to join him in his search.

But the preparations for the wedding of Perilaos and Anthia were going on apace, and it would have been consummated had not Anthia found a friend in an Ephesian physician Eudoxos to whom she confided her tragedy. She begged him to give her poison so that she might die faithful. She promised him silver so that he might return to Ephesus. Eudoxos gave her not poison but a sleeping potion, then hurriedly departed. The very night of her wedding, in the nuptial chamber, Anthia took what she believed poison. Perilaos coming to his bride found a corpse. To do her all honor, the bereft bridegroom had her placed in a magnificent tomb with splendid funeral gifts.

Robbers broke in the tomb for the treasure just as Anthia awoke. They carried her off with them to Alexandria. No one else knew she was alive. Habrocomes heard from an old woman the story of Anthia's death, of the pillaging of her tomb and the carrying off of her body. So leaving Hippothoos he started off alone by ship for Egypt hoping to find the brigands who had committed such sacrilege. The bandits had already sold Anthia to a rajah named Psammis, but Anthia saved herself from his amorousness by telling him that she was a consecrated priestess of Isis so he respected her.

Habrocomes' ship missed its course to Alexandria and

landed in Phoenicia. There the inhabitants set upon the strangers and capturing them sold them as slaves at Pelusium, Habrocomes to an old soldier, Araxos. This soldier had a hideous and wicked wife Cyno who, falling in love with Habrocomes, offered to kill her husband and marry him. When he refused, she herself killed her husband and accused Habrocomes of the murder. He was sent to Alexandria to be tried. Hippothoos meanwhile had gathered a new band and in his travels had come to Egypt and made the mountains near the frontiers of Ethiopia his center for expeditions. Habrocomes was condemned to death by the Prefect of Egypt, but his execution was twice frustrated by miracles caused by the Nile river when he appealed to the sun-god Helios for aid against injustice. So he was cast into prison.

At this time Psammis started home to India with a great camel train taking Anthia with him. At Memphis Anthia offered prayers to Isis begging her aid. As they neared the borders of Ethiopia, Hippothoos with his band fell upon their caravan and, slaying Psammis and many men, seized his treasure and took captive Anthia. Hippothoos and Anthia did not recognize each other.

The Prefect of Egypt, on giving Habrocomes a new hearing, was convinced of his innocence, freed him and gave him money. So Habrocomes took ship again and went to Italy to make inquiries there about Anthia. Cyno was executed.

Anthia was again in danger because of the lust of one of the bandits, Anchialos. He, while Hippothoos was away, tried to do violence to her, but she stabbed him fatally with a sword which she had found. Hippothoos on his return decided, in vengeance for the death of his companion, to kill her in a horrible way : to put her in a deep trench with two fierce dogs. But the bandit set to guard the trench from pity secretly conveyed food to her so that she fed and tamed the beasts.

Habrocomes on arriving at Syracuse in Sicily lived with a poor old fisherman named Aegialeus who treated him like a son and told him his own sad love-story. This is the story of the Mummy in the House. Hippothoos left Ethiopia to go to Alexandria and believing Anthia dead made no inquiries about her. The bandit left to guard her, now in love with her, hid in a cave with a good store of provisions until the caravan had gone, then released Anthia and the devoted dogs. He swore by the Sun and the gods of Egypt to respect her until she voluntarily came to his arms, so dogs and all they started on their travels.

The Prefect of Egypt had sent a company of soldiers under Polyidos to disperse the bandits of whose marauding he had heard. Hippothoos' band was broken up ; indeed he alone escaped. He embarked on a ship for Sicily. Polyidos next captured Anthia and her escort. Polyidos although he had a wife in Alexandria at once fell in love with Anthia and when they reached Memphis, tried to rape her, but she fled to the temple of Isis as a suppliant. Polyidos then swore that he would respect her if she would return to him, saying that to see her and speak to her would satisfy his love, so she went back to his care. On their arrival at Alexandria, Rhenaea the wife of Polyidos was nearly insane with jealousy of the girl her husband had brought home. One day in her husband's absence she beat and reviled poor Anthia, then gave her to a faithful slave with orders to take her to Italy and sell her there to a procurer. This he did at Taras.

Hippothoos by this time had reached Sicily and was staying at Tauromenium. Habrocomes at Syracuse in despair planned to go to Italy and if he found no news of Anthia there, to return to Ephesus. The parents of the young pair in their anxiety over them had died.   The slaves Leucon and Rhode who had been sold in Lycia had, on the death of their master, inherited his wealth.   They were on their way back to Ephesus but were staying at Rhodes.

The procurer now forced Anthia to stand in front of his brothel, magnificently arrayed, to attract customers. When many had gathered because of her beauty, Anthia feigned a seizure and fell down in the sight of all in convulsions.   Later when she declared to the procurer that she had had this malady since childhood, he treated her kindly.

Hippothoos in Tauromenium had come into great need. So when an elderly woman fell in love with him, constrained by poverty, he married her.   Very shortly she died, leaving him all her possessions.   So he set sail for Italy always hoping to find his dear Habrocomes.   Arriving at Taras he saw Anthia in the slave market where the procurer because of her illness was exhibiting her for sale. Hippothoos, recognizing her, learned from her lips her story, pitied her, bought her and offered her marriage. Finally Anthia told him that she was the wife of Habrocomes whom she had lost.   Hippothoos on hearing this revealed his devotion to Habrocomes and promised to help her find her husband.

Habrocomes also had come to Italy, but in despair had given up his quest and started back to Ephesus.   Stopping at Rhodes on his voyage he was discovered by Leucon and Rhode, who now took care of him.   Next Hippothoos also arrived at Rhodes, for he was taking Anthia back to Ephesus.   It was the time of a great festival to Helios.   At the temple Anthia dedicated locks of her hair with an inscription :

"In behalf of her husband Habrocomes Anthia dedicates her locks to the god."

This inscription was seen by Leucon and Rhode and the next day they found Anthia herself in the temple and told her that Habrocomes was alive and near and faithful. The good news spread through the city. A Rhodian carried the word to Habrocomes and he came running like a madman through the crowd, crying: "Anthia !" Near the temple of Isis he found her, and they fell into each other's arms. Then while the people cheered, they went into the temple of Isis and offered thanks to the goddess for their salvation. Then they went to the house of Leucon and at a banquet that night told all their adventures.

When at last Habrocomes and Anthia were got to bed, they assured each other that they had kept their oaths of faithfulness. The next day all sailed to Ephesus. There in the temple of Artemis Habrocomes and Anthia offered prayers and sacrifices ; also they put up an inscription telling what they had suffered and achieved. They erected magnificent sepulchres for their parents. And they passed the rest of their lives together as though every day were a festival. Leucon and Rhode shared all their happiness and Hippothoos too established himself in Ephesus to be near them.

From this summary of the plot, it is at once apparent that the chief interests of the romance are love, adventure and religion. The three are used by Xenophon with almost equal distribution of interest and emphasis. Two divinely beautiful young people (the lad only sixteen) fell in love with each other at first sight at the festival of Artemis. Habrocomes had been too proud of his appearance and in his arrogance had scorned the beautiful god of Love as his inferior. So Eros brought him low and made the pair suffer many misfortunes through separation. However they were married first and through all their troubles they were true to their oaths of mutual faithfulness. Temptations and adventures could not nullify their chastity, but their victories were often superhuman and made possible only by miracles and the aid of protecting gods. Anthia after a dream of seeing Habrocomes drawn away from her by another fair lady awoke to utter the belief that if he had broken faith, he had been forced by necessity ; and for herself she would die before losing her virtue.[6] At the end, when Anthia had proudly recounted the lovers she had escaped, Moeris, Perilaos, Psammis, Polyidos, Anchialos, the ruler of Taras, Habrocomes was able to reply that no other lady had ever seemed to him fair or desirable : his Anthia found him as she had left him in the prison at Tyre.[7] So hero and heroine shine as types of perfect virtue. The nobility of the romance, as Dalmeyda points out, appears not only in the purity of Habrocomes and Anthia, but in a restrained expression of the sentiments and the acts of love.[8]

The course of this true love was proverbially unsmooth and after the pair were separated, the plot seesaws between the adventures of hero and heroine. These are varied, exciting and often closely paralleled. Both were assailed by amorous lovers, Anthia by at least nine, Habrocomes by Corymbos, a pirate, by Manto, daughter of the chief of the pirate band, and by Cyno, the lewd wife of an old soldier. Both were shipwrecked, Anthia twice. Both nearly met death : Anthia as a human sacrifice, by taking poison, by being thrown in a trench with fierce dogs ; Habrocomes by crucifixion and pyre. Bandits and pirates captured both. Both were nearly executed for murder, Anthia for

[6] V. 8.
[7] V. 14.
[8] Dalmeyda, *op. cit.*, p. xxiii, for

example in the love-story of Aegialeus, V. 1, 4, for the climax : καὶ ἀπηλαύσομεν ὧν ἕνεκα συνήλθομεν.

actually killing a bandit who attacked her, Habrocomes on the false charge of Cyno.   Both were sold into slavery, Habrocomes once, Anthia over and over again.   Strangely enough among their adventures war played little part : the only wars described are official expeditions against bandits.

From most of these adventures the pair were saved by their piety.   Never did they lose an opportunity of offering prayer, thanksgiving, vows and sacrifices to the gods. The story begins with the festival of Artemis at Ephesus at which Habrocomes and Anthia fell in love and ends with their return to her temple to offer thanksgiving for a happy ending out of all their misfortunes.   At the festival Anthia appeared as the priestess of Artemis and led a procession of maidens in which she alone was garbed as Artemis.   This may be a symbol of her resolute chastity. Many details of the worship of the goddess are given which seem based on reality.[9]   Artemis appears not as the Ephesian goddess of fertility, but as the protectress of chastity and in this function joins with Isis in safeguarding the purity of the heroine.

Eros is the offended god who undoubtedly in vengeance caused the violent love of Habrocomes, the separation and the miseries of the unhappy pair.   There are few references to Aphrodite : to her son rather than to herself is given the function of inspiring love.   On the Babylonian baldequin over the marriage bed of Habrocomes and Anthia there had been woven a scene in which Aphrodite appeared attended by little Loves and Ares unarmed was coming towards her led by Eros bearing a lighted torch.[10] Habrocomes at Cyprus offered prayers to Aphrodite.[11]

The oracle of Apollo at Claros determined the plot by

---

[9] Dalmeyda, *op. cit.*, pp. xvi–xviii ;   [10] I. 8.
Calderini, *op. cit.*, p. 85.   [11] V. 10.

ordering the marriage of Habrocomes and Anthia and predicting their voyaging, their separation, their disasters, their reunion. But its clauses are not sufficiently explained : we are never told why the young bride and groom and their parents feel they must start out on their fateful journey. Some think the obscurity is due to Xenophon's epitomizer. There are other possible explanations. The action may be an abandoning of themselves to the will of the gods ; or a bold step towards their final promised safety ; or a flight from the city where they had suffered so much. An oracle is the traditional prelude to a voyage of adventure. Xenophon uses it, says Dalmeyda, to pique curiosity, to render the misfortunes of the two more dramatic by the prophecy of them and to reassure his readers about a happy ending.[12]

In happiness or distress both the young lovers honored the god of the place in which they found themselves. In the first part of their journey together they offered sacrifice to Hera in her sanctuary at Samos.[13] At Rhodes, Habrocomes' prayer to Helios saved him from crucifixion and burning through the miracles of the Nile.[14] Perhaps Helios was rewarding Habrocomes for the golden armor which he and Anthia had jointly dedicated to him at Rhodes in his temple.[15] This votive had another certain part in the plot because when Habrocomes returned there alone to pray near his votive, Leucon and Rhode, who had been reading the inscription set up near it by their masters, recognized him and revealed themselves.[16] At Memphis Anthia appealing to the pity of the god Apis received from his famous oracle a promise that she would find Habrocomes.[17]

Ares appears only in Xenophon. This is strange when

12 Dalmeyda, *op. cit.*, pp. xxiv–xxv.　　15 I. 12.
13 I. 11.　　　　　　　　　　　　　　　16 V. 10–11.
14 IV. 2.　　　　　　　　　　　　　　　17 V. 4.

war plays such a part in the other romances.   In the
Ephesiaca, Hippothoos and his bandits at the festival of
Ares had the custom of suspending the victim to be sacrificed, human being or animal, from a tree and killing it by
hurling their javelins at it.   They were preparing to sacrifice Anthia in this way when she was rescued.[18]

The other cult which is as important as that of Artemis
for the story is the cult of Isis.   Anthia saved herself from
Psammis' advances by declaring that she was a consecrated
priestess of Isis so the rajah respected her person.[19]   At
Memphis in her temple, Anthia appealed to Isis who had
preserved her chastity in the past to grant her salvation and
restore her to Habrocomes.[20]   To escape Polyidos' lust,
Anthia took refuge at the sanctuary of Isis at Memphis and
again besought the goddess for aid.   Polyidos in fear of
Isis and pity for Anthia promised to respect her.[21]   Finally
near that temple of Isis Habrocomes and Anthia found
each other and in the same temple they offered prayers of
thanksgiving.[22]   Isis thus in the *Ephesiaca* figures as the
protectress of chastity.

The worship of Isis had been carried to the coast of Asia
Minor by sailors and traders.   In the empire both Artemis and Isis had statues in the Artemesion of Ephesus.
The Egyptian cult, purified and penetrated with moral
ideas, seems to belong to the second century A.D.   From
its very nature, the goddess Isis becomes as natural a pro-
tector of Anthia as is Artemis.[23]   This synthesis of the
two goddesses in one protectress of the heroine is a natural
process of the philosophical thought of the time.   In a
modern novel or a cinema, better clarity would be attained
for our non-philosophical minds if one goddess, Isis, was
worshipped by Anthia and was the deity of her salvation.

18 II. 13 ; III. 3.   21 V. 4.
19 III. 11–12.   22 V. 13.
20 IV. 3.   23 Dalmeyda, *op. cit.,* pp. xvi–xviii.

Apuleius achieved just this simplification in his novel by making Isis the one and only savior of his hero Lucius.

To develop and sustain these three main interests of the story, love, adventure and religion, the usual devices of a plot are employed. The setting is cinematic in its many changes : Ephesus, the ocean, Samos, Rhodes, Tyre, Syria, Cilicia, Cappadocia, Egypt, Sicily, Italy, Rhodes again, back to Ephesus, and thrown in with the setting are many geographical details which are often wrong.[24] The characters are familiar types : the ravishingly beautiful hero and heroine, their perturbed parents, high officials (Perilaos and Psammis) who take the place of historical characters, faithful slaves, a wily procurer, a doctor, pirates, bandits.

Dalmeyda has written a discriminating paragraph on the morality of the characters.[25] He says that of course all the characters of the romance do not attain the perfection of virtue of the two protagonists, but altogether the author shows us a gallery of persons without wickedness who are sympathetic and who have an air of honesty even in the exercise of the worst occupations. Manto, who falsely accuses Habrocomes of having wished to violate her and who has him cruelly tortured, is motivated by an overwhelming passion. Apsyrtos, her father, chief of the pirates, shows himself just and generous to the hero when he has discovered his daughter's calumny. The slaves are devoted and faithful. Lampon to whom Manto gives Anthia as his wife is a rustic full of civility and goodness. The man who traffics in young girls to whom Anthia is sold shows a noble sympathy when she pretends to be afflicted with seizures. Hippothoos, a brigand chief, exercises his trade ruthlessly putting villages to fire and sword ; he has a weakness too for handsome lads ; but to Habroc-

[24] Calderini, *op. cit.*, pp. 120-25.   [25] Dalmeyda, *op. cit.*, pp. xviii-xxiv.

omes he is a faithful and devoted friend. He renounces his passion for Anthia when he finds she is the wife of his friend and aids her in every way in her search for Habrocomes. It is this recognition of some good in every human being that gives Xenophon his large humanity.

Oracles are given by Apollo at Claros and by Apis in Memphis. Dreams and visions disturb both hero and heroine. A letter (Manto's) is important for the plot. Some conversation is used. A court-room scene is sketched in, Habrocomes' trial for murder before the prefect of Egypt. Soliloquies are frequent since woeful lovers parted must bewail their lot. Attempted suicides testify to their despair.[26] Résumés of adventures are helpfully presented by important characters at different stages in the narrative. And after a hundred hair-breadth escapes, journeys end in lovers' meetings as the oracle of Apollo had reassuringly predicted at the beginning of the romance.

In spite of the use of these conventions, the story has a lively and compelling interest. We are led to share the admiration and marvel of the characters themselves. We are moved by the pity which they often feel. Their piety induces in us reverence. We agree with their preference for Greeks rather than barbarians. And we admire the romantic love which maintains faithfulness in the face of death, or outlives death itself.[27]

The style of this gem of a novel is finely cut, clear and beautiful in its pure Atticism. Dalmeyda, who follows Rohde and Bürger in believing the present form of the romance is due to an epitomizer, yet has to admit that all the "naked simplicity" of the style is not due to the redactor.[28] This characteristic is so distinctive of the au-

---

[26] Calderini, *op. cit.*, p. 113. [28] Dalmeyda, *op. cit.*, p. xxvii.
[27] See the story of the old Spartan and his mummy, V. 1.

thor that it seems to differentiate him from other writers of
romance by giving his story the air of a popular tale.
Sometimes, Dalmeyda continues, the expression is double,
as if in a sort of naive elegance. Words are repeated awk-
wardly. Stereotyped formulae are used. The author
gives every person a name even if he appears only once.
Love is generally expressed in conventional terms, which
are however intended to suggest its violent or tragic character. There is even a ready-made formula for ecstasy
(οὐκέτι καρτερῶν or οὐκέτι φέρειν δυνάμενος). But the passion of
Habrocomes and Anthia is expressed differently. At their
final reunion Xenophon describes with force and delicacy
their joy which is both tender and passionate.[29]

Whether "the naked simplicity" of the *Ephesiaca* is to
be attributed to an epitomizer, to its approach to the genre
of a popular tale, or to the author's own taste, the romance
is certainly characterized throughout by brevity, restraint
and sparcity of decoration. There are so few descriptions
that those of the festival of Artemis and of the canopy over
the marriage bed of Habrocomes and Anthia are notable.[30]
The action is too rapid and varied to allow time for decorative passages. Instead of being set amid purple patches,
it is advanced by a kind of documentary evidence : two
oracles, two letters, one memorial and two votive inscriptions, all directly quoted,[31] and a reference to an inscription finally offered as a votive in the Artemesion by Habrocomes and Anthia giving an account of all their adventures.

Inset narratives, those stories within stories which make
pleasing digressions in other longer romances, are here
very few. Hippothoos recounts his love for the beautiful

---

[29] Dalmeyda, *op. cit.*, pp. xxviii–
ix.
[30] I. 2 ; I. 8.

[31] I. 6, V. 4 ; II. 1, II. 12 ; III. 2,
I. 12, V. 11.

Hyperanthes and the boy's untimely drowning.[32]   Aegialeus, the Spartan living with the mummy of his wife, tells how his love for her has outlasted death.[33]   Both these narratives are colorful, dramatic and poignant from the very qualities which characterize all the romance.   These are brevity, sincerity and restrained emotion.

The influence of Chariton is clearly seen in Xenophon both in direct imitation and in qualities of style.   When the Phoenician pirates had kidnapped Habrocomes and Anthia on their trireme and fired their captives' vessel leaving many to perish in the sea, an old slave, as he swam, pitifully called to Habrocomes to save his aged paedagogue or at least kill him and bury him.[34]   In view of the situation this is a ridiculous appeal, but it is a clear imitation of a passage in Chariton where, when Chaereas resolves to go to sea to search for Callirhoe, his father Ariston begs his son not to desert him, but to take him on his trireme,[35] or to wait a few days for his father's death and burial. Anthia, when Manto, the daughter of the brigand chief, demands Habrocomes' submission to her passion, begs her husband to save his life in this way and swears that she will leave him free by killing herself, only asking from him burial, one last kiss, and a place in his memory.   This is in direct imitation of Chariton and of Chaereas' words when he finds Callirhoe married to Dionysius.[36]   Here Xenophon is simpler than his model, for he does not transfer the effective lines from Homer which Chariton quotes.[37] The burial of Anthia with its rich funeral gifts resembles the burial of Callirhoe and also the lavish equipment of the cenotaph for Chaereas.[38]   The language of Chariton

[32] V. 15.
[33] V. 1.
[34] I. 14.
[35] Chariton, III. 5.   See Dalmeyda, *op. cit.*, p. xxx.

[36] II. 4.   Chariton, V. 10.
[37] *Iliad*, XXII, 389–90 ; Dalmeyda, *op. cit.*, p. xxix.
[38] III. 7 ; Chariton, I. 6 ; IV. 1.

is adapted for the lament of Habrocomes in Italy at the failure of his quest and his renewed pledge of faithfulness unto death.[39]

These clear indications of imitation of detail serve to corroborate the evidence of general imitation of style. Indeed Dalmeyda sees in the whole temperament of Xenophon a close affinity to Chariton. Xenophon introduces the most startling events without fanfare. Characteristic of his style are accumulated questions, pathetic résumés, oaths, invocations of the gods, apostrophes of men and of things particularly of that fatal beauty which the young hero and heroine deplore because of their misery. Xenophon's relation to Chariton in all this is striking.[40]

The plot of the novel has seemed to some critics epic in its chronological narrative of successive adventures. Others find the structure a tragic plot with an angry god demanding satisfaction for the sin of arrogance and the guilty hero involving in his own nemesis the one most dear to him. It is true that this and other resemblances to tragedy exist. The story of Manto and her false denunciation of Habrocomes for an attempt to rape her after she has failed to win his love goes back to the Phaedra story of Euripides' *Hippolytus*. The noble goatherd husband of Anthia finds his prototype in Electra's peasant husband in Euripides' play. The scene where Anthia on her wedding-night takes poison which proves to be a sleeping potion, to avoid a new marriage and keep her troth to her lost love seems to be the antecedent of the poison scene in Shakespeare's *Romeo and Juliet*.

To me, however, this novelette finds its closest affiliation in another successor. Both the structure and the devices used to arouse emotion anticipate the modern cinema. This contemporary form of amusement is such an accepted

---

[39] V. 8 ; Chariton, V. 10.   [40] Dalmeyda, *op. cit.*, pp. xxxii–iii.

part of modern life that we hardly need to read the books about the cinema by Allerdyce Nicoll, Lewis Jacobs, Maurice Bardèche and others to understand "the Rise of the American Film." Personally I go to the movies to escape from routine and from painful thoughts of our own times. Occasionally I allow myself to be educated about *Steel* or *The River*. I prefer to industrial films or films of social problems like lynching, prison conditions, housing, films with biographies of great historical characters : Pasteur, Zola, Rembrandt. I like films set in local history such as *Maryland* or *Kentucky* or *Gone with the Wind* or *The Howards of Virginia* or *The North West Mounted Police*. I have to shut my eyes during the fighting and the cruelties of *Sea Hawk* and *All This and Heaven Too*. But I like the cinematic rapidity of changes of scene, the control by the camera of space and magnitude, the extension of the time-limit, the fade-ins and fade-outs which can create fantastic visions, the value of the flash-back to recall what has been already seen, the concentration of interest achieved by close-ups.

Many of these devices I recognize in the Greek Romances and especially in Xenophon of Ephesus. His narrative is as condensed as that of a scenario with lacunae, abrupt transitions, failures in an adequate vocabulary of emotion. The local history of Ephesus is emphasized and depicted. Scenes shift with cinematic rapidity. Hair-raising adventures succeed each other at an exciting pace. Bandits and pirates achieve robbery and kidnapping. High police officials or officers like G-Men perform valiant rescues. Court-room scenes as in many films vie with shipwrecks in interest. Documents like letters are presented to the reader's eye as on the screen. Visions and dreams are made to seem as real as in fade-ins and fade-outs.

There is a clear morality in the opposition of good and

bad characters and in the final victory of the good.   Hero
and heroine captivate by their extraordinary beauty and
maintain their chastity and fidelity against terrific odds.
Hence their phenomenal virtue is rewarded by reunion in
the end.   Religion often plays a saving part (as on the
screen for example in *Brother Orchid*).   The Reader like
the audience at the movie goes away with a sense of having
been enlivened, entertained and vastly improved.   For
the function of the Greek romance in the second and third
centuries A.D., when the universal rule of the Roman Empire gave scant scope for great oratory or tragedy under
the blessings of an enforced peace, was to entertain and to
edify.   The Greek romance substituted for the adventures
of the mind new themes : the excitements of passion, the
interests of travel, and the consolations of religion.   It was
lifted out of the ranks of the trivial and the second-rate by
its great central theme : that there is such a thing as true
love ; that weighed in the balance against it all the world
is nothing ; and that it outlives time and even death.

Our own age in America, bleeding internally from the
agony of a war which it is powerless to end, fearful for its
own menaced security, demands from the cinema not only
temporary oblivion and excitement, but encouragement
to believe that love lasts even unto death, that heroes ride
again and are victorious, and that finally, by the help of
God, the right will conquer.

IV

THE AETHIOPICA *OF HELIODORUS*

THE life of Heliodorus is as obscure as that of each of the
other writers of Greek romance, but in the tradition of
his there is a special point of controversy. Was Heliodorus a pagan novelist or a Christian bishop ? Or by some
strange metamorphosis did the writer of the romantic
Aethiopica become in later and staider years the Bishop of
Tricca ? The only certain facts are found in the autobio-
graphical sentence which concludes the romance, that he
was a Phoenician of Emesa, of a family descended from
Helios, the son of Theodosius.

It was Socrates who, in the fifth century A.D., stated that
the custom of celibacy for the clergy was introduced in
Thessaly by Heliodorus when he became bishop of Tricca.
He added that Heliodorus wrote in his youth a love-story,
which he called *Aethiopica*.[1] Photius in the ninth century says that he received the bishopric later, that is after
writing the romance. Nicephorus Callistus in the four-
teenth century after quoting the remark of Socrates adds
that the *Aethiopica* created such a scandal Heliodorus had
to choose between his bishopric and the destruction of his
romance so he abandoned his charge, but this is probably
mere embellishment of the story. As Rattenbury points

[1] For this introduction to Heliodorus I am largely indebted to the edition
of *Les Éthiopiques* edited by R. M. Rattenbury. T. W. Lumb, J. Maillon,
Paris, vol. I, 1935 ; vol. II, 1938. For the *Testimonia* see *Heliodori Aethiopica*
by Aristides Colonna, Rome, 1938, pp. 361–72.

out,[2] neither Socrates, Photius nor Nicephorus declares that Heliodorus was a Christian when he wrote his romance, but they imply clearly that he became a bishop afterwards. And if the author of the romance was a devout pagan as he seems to have been, that state of mind could have made possible his conversion to Christianity. This seems a reasonable explanation of the strong tradition continuing from the fifth century that Heliodorus became bishop of Tricca.

As to his date, there are some certainties but no exactitude. The Bishop of Tricca must have lived before Socrates wrote his *Historia Ecclesiastica* which covered the period 306–439. There is no external evidence on the time of the writer of the romance, but from the general conclusions about the dating of the Greek Romances, he probably wrote not later than the end of the third century. His native city Emesa was the birthplace of two Roman Emperors, Heliogabalus (218–222) and Alexander Severus (222–235). About the middle of the century Emesa was conquered by Zenobia of Palmyra, but was freed by Aurelian in 272. Heliodorus may have written in its most flourishing period, 220–240. It is generally agreed that Heliodorus is later than Chariton who could not have written after 150 and earlier than Achilles Tatius who wrote about the beginning of the fourth century.

Rattenbury thinks that a possible reconstruction of Heliodorus' life is this. He was born in Emesa in Phoenician Syria. His family was connected with the cult of the Sun. In his youth, perhaps between 220 and 240, he wrote a romance in which the influence of the cult of Helios appears, also the neo-Pythagoreanism of Apollonius of Tyana. It is not impossible that finally he was converted to Christianity, became bishop of Tricca and in that office

[2] R. M. Rattenbury, T. W. Lumb, J. Maillon, *op. cit.*, I, ix–xi.

introduced in his diocese celibacy for the clergy.[3] Calderini has shown with discrimination and perspicacity
that the special characteristic of the *Aethiopica* is the interest in philosophy which distinguishes it and its author
from Chariton, the writer of historical romance, and from
Achilles Tatius, the writer of romance tinged with science.[4] A study of the *Aethiopica* itself will show how
deeply infused the novel is with this religious philosophical coloring.

Before outlining the narrative, I will give as usual a list
of the principal characters.   These are :

Theagenes, the young Greek hero
Chariclea, the young heroine, supposed to be a Greek
Hydaspes, king of Ethiopia
Persinna, queen of Ethiopia
Calasiris, of Memphis, priest of Isis and his sons :
    Thyamis, in exile, a pirate captain
    Petosiris, priest of Isis
Charicles, priest of Apollo at Delphi
Alcamenes, nephew of Charicles
Trachinus, a pirate
Pelorus, a pirate and officer of Trachinus
Cnemon, a young Athenian, son of
Aristippus, an Athenian, a stupid husband
Demaeneta, the amorous step-mother of Cnemon
Thisbe, the scheming maid of Demaeneta
Arsinoe, a slave-girl, a friend of Thisbe
Nausicles, a merchant
Thermuthis, an officer under Thyamis
Oroondates, viceroy of the Great King of the Persians
Mithranes, viceroy of Oroondates
Arsace, wife of Oroondates
Cybele, the maid of Arsace
Achaemenes, son of Cybele
Euphrates, the chief eunuch of Oroondates
Sisimithres, an Ethiopian Gymnosophist
Meroebus, nephew of Hydaspes

[3] R. M. Rattenbury, T. W. Lumb,
J. Maillon, *op. cit.,* I, xiii–xv.

[4] Aristide Calderini, *Le Avventure
di Cherea e Calliroe,* Torino, 1913,
pp. 176–77.

The opening scene of the romance is startling and mysterious. In Egypt, from a mountain near the mouth of the Nile a band of pirates get a view of the seashore. They behold a heavily laden ship without a crew, a plain strewn with dead bodies and the remains of an ill-fated banquet. A wounded youth is lying on the ground. He is being cared for by a beautiful young woman dressed in a religious garb which makes her seem a priestess or a goddess, Diana or Isis. Indeed a divine effulgence emanates from her. The pirates though at first overawed descend and collect rich booty. Their captain then courteously conveys the maiden and the youth to their pirate home. This was called "The Pasture" and was a sort of island in a delta of the Nile. Some of the pirates lived in huts made of reeds, some in boats. The water was their fortification. Their streets were winding water-ways cut through the reeds.

The pirate chief assigned the care of his two captives to a young Greek, Cnemon, who was his interpreter. The prisoners were overjoyed on finding their custodian a Greek. He promised to heal the wounds of Theagenes, who had now revealed his own name and that of Chariclea, and on their urgent request, he told him his own story.

"I," he said, "am the son of Aristippus, an Athenian. After my brother's death, my father married again a woman named Demaeneta, who was a mischief-maker. Like Phaedra she fell in love with me, her step-son, indeed called me her dear Hippolytus. When I repelled her advances she accused me to my father of attempted rape. He had me scourged. Worse than that, Thisbe, the maid of Demaeneta, on her mistress' orders involved me in an amorous intrigue with herself and later promised to show me my step-mother with an adulterer. Sword in hand I

followed her to the bed-room and just as I was about to
murder her paramour, I found he was my father. Aristippus charged me in court with attempted parricide.
Only a divided vote spared my life and sent me into exile.
Lately I received news that my father through Thisbe had
found out his wife's corruption ; she had killed herself ;
and now Aristippus is trying to obtain from the people his
son's pardon."

The next day Thyamis the pirate leader although he
was warned in a dream that having Chariclea, he would
not have her, announced to his band his intention of
marrying her. She pretended to consent, but asked that
their marriage be postponed until they reached Memphis
so that there she could resign her priesthood of Diana.
Thyamis accepted this condition. Theagenes was horrified until Chariclea explained that this agreement was
made only to secure more time for their plans for safety.
A hostile band of brigands was now seen approaching.
Thyamis had Cnemon hide Chariclea in a secret cave.
When the terrible battle began to go against him, Thyamis
rushed back to the cave and killed a woman in the dark
whom he believed Chariclea. In battle he was then taken
alive. The victorious brigands fired the huts on the island but did not find the cave. Cnemon and Theagenes,
who had escaped in little boats, returned to the island.
When Cnemon conducted Theagenes to the cave by its
secret entrance, they found in its dark gloom the body of
a dead woman. Theagenes believing it Chariclea burst
into lamentation and planned suicide. But Cnemon took
away his sword, got a torch lighted and found that the
woman was Thisbe and in her dead hand was a letter.
They soon found Chariclea alive.

After the first joy of reunion Chariclea wished to know

who the dead woman was.   Cnemon revealed that she was Thisbe and related all her story : how after her plot against him, Arsinoe, a rival courtesan whose lover Nausicles she had stolen, revealed Thisbe's machinations against Demaeneta ; how Cnemon's father was exiled on the ground of complicity and Thisbe fled.   The letter in Thisbe's hand proved to be to Cnemon, a petition to save her from the pirates who had stolen her.   Just then Thermuthis, her pirate captor, arrived to reclaim her, only to find her dead.   The sword in her wound proved to him that she was slain by Thyamis.

Theagenes and Chariclea, Cnemon and Thermuthis now started out in separate pairs towards Chemmis, a rich city on the Nile, to get food.   The menace of Thermuthis was conveniently removed as he died from the bite of an asp.   Near Chemmis Cnemon met an old man who entertained him at his home.   He proved to be Calasiris, the foster-father of Theagenes and Chariclea.   This he revealed to Cnemon in a long narrative of his own life : how though a priest of Isis he had gone into voluntary exile to break off the wiles of a courtesan ; how he had sojourned at Delphi, attending the ceremonies and talking with the philosophers.   One, Charicles, related how in his own travels in Egypt he had had intrusted to him by an Ethiopian merchant a beautiful child.   The merchant had found her exposed with a bag of jewels and an inscribed fillet.   These too he gave to Charicles making him promise to guard her freedom and wed her to a free man.   He had named her Chariclea and brought her up in Greece but now, though she was very beautiful, she refused to marry.

Calasiris also described to Cnemon the sacrifice to Neoptolemus offered by the Aenianians and the Delphic oracle which he had heard there.

"Delphians, regard with reverential care,
Both him the goddess-born, and her the fair ;
"Grace" is the sound which ushers in her name,
The syllable wherewith it ends, is *"Fame."*
They both my fane shall leave, and oceans past,
In regions torrid shall arrive at last ;
There shall the gods reward their pious vows,
And snowy chaplets bind their dusky brows." [5]

Calasiris at the urgent request of Cnemon described all
the ceremonies attendant on the sacrifice to Neoptolemus : the hecatomb and the other victims, the Thracian
maidens bearing offerings, the hymn to the Hero, the
dance, the procession of the fifty armed horsemen led by
Theagenes, the radiant appearance of Chariclea in a chariot. All this description was the brilliant setting for the
meeting of Theagenes and Chariclea, for when Theagenes
took from the priestess' hand the torch to light the sacrifi-
cial pyre, in them both the flame of first love was kindled.

The next day Chariclea lay abed very ill in her apartment in the temple. Calasiris feared it was due to *"fas-
cinatio."* Calasiris after meeting Theagenes had a vision
in which Apollo and Diana consigned Theagenes and
Chariclea to his care and bade him take them to Egypt.
The next morning Theagenes confessed to Calasiris his
love and besought his aid. Charicles begged him to heal
his daughter. This enabled him to talk to her.

Chariclea recovered sufficiently the next day to attend
the contest of the men in armor and to award the palm to
the victor, Theagenes. But her passion and her illness
increased after this second meeting and Calasiris was
again summoned to treat her. Her disease was diagnosed
as love and Calasiris persuaded her father to let him see

[5] II. 35, translated by the Rev. Rowland Smith, in *The Greek Romances of
Heliodorus, Longus, and Achilles Tatius*, London, 1855, pp. 61–62. It is
impossible to reproduce in English the Greek's hidden references to the
names of Chariclea, Famed-for-her-Grace, and of Theagenes, the Goddess-
Born.

the fillet found with the exposed baby.   Calasiris was able to read the inscription on it.   It was a letter from her mother, Persinna, queen of the Ethiopians, revealing that she had borne a white daughter because at her conception she had been looking at a picture of Andromeda ; then fearing the charge of adultery she had exposed her baby with the fillet and the jewels.   All this Calasiris told to Chariclea.   Calasiris then made a plot with her by which she was to pretend to become affianced to Alcamenes, the nephew of Charicles, as her foster-father wished.   Charicles was delighted although he was nervous because of a dream in which an eagle from the hand of Apollo bore his daughter away.   He gave her all the jewels.

Then Calasiris persuaded some Phoenician merchants to take him and two friends on their ship as far as Sicily ; and he ordered Theagenes and his young friends to kidnap Chariclea.   She consented to the plan after Theagenes had bound himself by an oath never to force her love. After they were off, Charicles roused the city to pursuit of them.   Calasiris after telling of the arrival of the Phoenician ship at Zacynthos interrupted his narrative to rest. Nausicles returned to the house and unknown to the others had brought Chariclea with him.

(Here the author himself gave a résumé of the adventures of Theagenes and Chariclea from the time they parted with Cnemon.   In the cave the lovers had a long talk and made an agreement as to what they would do in case fortune again separated them : they would inscribe on temple, statue, herm or boundary stone, Theagenes the name Pythicus, Chariclea Pythias ; the direction in which each departed ; to what place or people ; also the time of writing.   For recognition if they met disguised they decided to use as signs Chariclea's ring and Theagenes' scar from a boar.   Their watchwords were to be a

lamp for her, a palm-tree for him. They sealed this cove-
nant in kisses, then left the cave taking Chariclea's sacred
robes, her bow and quiver and her jewels.

Soon they met an armed band and were taken prisoners.
The commander was Mithranes, an officer of Oroondates,
viceroy of Egypt. Nausicles had persuaded him for pay
to make this expedition to the island in search of his
Thisbe. Nausicles on seeing Theagenes and Chariclea
cleverly pretended that Chariclea was Thisbe, the object
of his quest. Mithranes demanded Theagenes as his prize
and despatched him to Oroondates as a fine youth for service with the Great King.)

The next day Calasiris and Cnemon heard all Nausicles'
story from himself, saw Chariclea and made a plan to ransom Theagenes. After Nausicles had celebrated a sacrifice in the temple of Hermes, the god of gain, Calasiris on
request continued his narrative of the voyage from Delphi.
At Zacynthos a deaf old fisherman Tyrrhenus gave them
lodging. The Tyrian merchant who won the victory at
the Pythian games now sued for Chariclea's hand. Tyrrhenus discovered an ambush of pirates waiting for the
Phoenician ship to sail. Calasiris without revealing this
persuaded the Tyrian captain to sail that night. The pirate crew under Trachinus pursued them and engaged
them in a terrible battle so finally the Phoenicians had to
surrender. Trachinus demanded marriage with Chariclea and she deceitfully promised her hand if he would
spare Calasiris and "her brother" Theagenes. With difficulty the pirates maneuvered the boat to land near the
mouth of the Nile. Trachinus told Calasiris that he proposed to marry Chariclea that day. Calasiris, ingenious as
ever, persuaded him to let Chariclea go on the ship to attire
herself for the wedding and be left undisturbed there.
Calasiris then plotted with Pelorus, second in command of

the pirates, telling him Chariclea loved him. Pelorus since he had been the first to board the Phoenician ship demanded, as his right of first choice of the booty, the girl. A terrible battle ensued in which Trachinus was killed, Pelorus wounded by Theagenes and put to flight and Theagenes badly wounded. In the morning Egyptian pirates arrived and carried them both off. Calasiris had spent his days mourning for them until this present recovery of Chariclea.

The next day Calasiris, Cnemon and Nausicles set out to find Theagenes. An acquaintance informed Nausicles that Mithranes had sent his troops on an expedition against the men of Bessa, commanded by Thyamis, because they had stolen a captive Greek youth. So Nausicles and his friends returned to Chemmis and told all to Chariclea. Nausicles gave a farewell dinner-party since the season favorable for navigation compelled him to sail for Greece Cnemon after a struggle with himself decided to go with him and was permitted to marry his daughter, Nausiclea.

Calasiris and Chariclea disguised as beggars started for Bessa to seek Theagenes. Near Bessa they found many corpses lying on the ground. An old woman told them there had been a battle between Mithranes' forces and the men of Bessa in which the men of Bessa had been victorious and Mithranes had been killed. The victors had now set out to Memphis against Oroondates. The old woman had lost her son in battle. That night Calasiris and Chariclea secretly watched her magic rites by which she raised him to give her news of her other son. The shade also revealed that there were two witnesses to her wicked necromancy ; that Chariclea should be happily reunited with Theagenes and that his own mother would meet her death by the sword. This soon happened, for she fell on an upright sword on the battle-field.

Calasiris and Chariclea arrived at Memphis just as Thyamis and his brigands began a siege of it. The people of Memphis in the absence of Oroondates consulted the queen Arsace about the wisdom of going out to attack the enemy. Thyamis had been driven into exile by the slanders of his brother Petosiris who swore there was an amour between Thyamis and Arsace. Petosiris had then succeeded his brother in the priesthood of Isis. Arsace after looking at the enemy from the wall ordered a single combat between Thyamis and Petosiris to decide the war. In this combat Petosiris was forced to flee. As he was running around the city walls the third time, Calasiris arrived and saw the combat between his two sons that an oracle had foretold. Rushing between them he ended the contest.

Chariclea discovered Theagenes and suddenly threw her arms about him. Her hero disgusted at her beggar's rags threw her off and did not recognize her until she whispered : "Pythias, have you forgotten the torch?" Then he took her to his arms, while Arsace and the other watchers on the wall marvelled at the scene as though it were on the stage. So peace was made by the father and the lovers were reunited. All went to the temple of Isis. Calasiris restored his son Thyamis to the priesthood.

Arsace had fallen madly in love with Theagenes on seeing him twice and confided this to her aged maid, Cybele. This maid on going to the temple of Isis to offer prayers for her mistress learned that Calasiris had died there during the night and that no one except the priests could enter the temple for seven days on account of the funeral rites. Thereupon Cybele craftily secured permission to entertain the two young Greeks who were staying there in Arsace's palace and took them home. When they found that they were in the palace, they became suspicious for they had noticed the queen's interest in Theagenes the day before. So at Chariclea's suggestion, Theagenes said they were brother and sister. Cybele went to Arsace's apartment to tell her all, locking the guests in their room. In her absence, her son Achaemenes came home, listened at their door and from their talk and from a glimpse at Theagenes realized that this was the very youth who had been taken from him by Thyamis.

As the days passed, Arsace tried to win the love of Theagenes first through subtle allurement, then through open confession of her passion and at last through domination. Achaemenes finally told Arsace who they were so the queen informed Theagenes that they were now her slaves as they had been the captive slaves of Mithranes and he must obey her. Then in the presence of Cybele Theagenes promised himself to Arsace on condition that she would never give Chariclea to Achaemenes, who had demanded her. He confessed that Chariclea was not his sister but his fiancée. On hearing this Achaemenes rode away to inform Oroondates of all.

Oroondates was engaged in a campaign against Hydaspes, King of the Ethiopians, who had got possession of Philae. On hearing Achaemenes' report Oroondates despatched his eunuch Bagoas with fifty horsemen to Memphis to bring Theagenes and Chariclea to his camp. He sent two letters to this effect to Arsace and to his chief eunuch. Achaemenes he kept with himself.

In Memphis Thyamis had been unable to procure the release of the young Greeks from Arsace. Moreover the frustrated queen had begun to try imprisonment and torture on Theagenes. When he was still obstinate, Cybele advised getting rid of Chariclea to free his heart and she prepared to poison the girl. Fortunately a maid exchanged the goblets. Cybele herself drank the poison

and expired, but with her last breath she declared Chariclea had murdered her.   So Arsace threw the girl into the
prison where Theagenes was and had her tried.   In the
court-room Chariclea pleaded guilty, for this was the plan
that she and her lover had agreed on in the prison, that
they might die together.   The Supreme Council ordered
that she be burned alive.   Chariclea was saved by a miracle, for the flames on the pyre refused to touch her person.   Arsace then consigned her again to prison on the
ground that she was a witch.

In prison, Chariclea and Theagenes had a long talk
about the dream-visions they had each seen.   To each
Calasiris had appeared and given a metrical prophecy.
To Chariclea he had said :

> "Bearing Pantarbè, fear not flames, fair maid,
> Fate, to whom naught is hard, shall bring thee aid."

And to Theagenes :

> "From Arsace, the morrow sets thee free —
> To Aethiopia with the virgin flee." [6]

Chariclea interpreted these oracles to mean that her jewel,
the Pantarbè, was protecting her ; and that on the next
day they would be freed from Arsace and go to Ethiopia.

Meanwhile Bagoas arrived at Memphis and Euphrates
on receiving the letter of Oroondates sent Theagenes and
Chariclea off secretly with Bagoas.   On their journey they
received first the news that Arsace had killed herself and
second that Oroondates had gone to Syene.   Later on the
way they were seized by a band of Troglodite Ethiopians
who took Bagoas and the two Greeks to their king, Hydaspes.   He planned to save them as victims to be sacrificed to the gods.

Hydaspes was besieging Syene.   Oroondates had got in-

[6] Translated by the Rev. Rowland Smith, *op. cit.*, pp. 196–97.

side the city before the blockade and was directing the defense. But Hydaspes used a new weapon against him, inundation. His army dug a great trench around Syene with earth-works encircling it. This trench he connected with the river Nile by a long canal, fifty feet wide, banked by high walls. When the works were finished, he cut away the embankment between his canal and the Nile and let the river in. Syene became an island city and the pressure of the water on the walls threatened inundation. So Oroondates and the people of Syene had to sue for peace. This was granted, and Hydaspes built up again the embankment between his canal and the Nile and proceeded to drain off the water.

During the festival of the overflowing of the Nile Oroondates and his army slipped away in the night, bridging the mud swamps about Syene by planks, and went to Elephantine, which revolted with him against Hydaspes. In the new battle Hydaspes was again victorious and took Oroondates prisoner, but the Ethiopian was a generous conqueror and sent Oroondates back to be again viceroy of his province.

Hydaspes on his way home stopped two days at Philae and from there sent home letters announcing his victory to Persinna and the Gymnosophists. Persinna recalled a dream that she had brought forth a full-grown daughter and interpreted the daughter as this victory. The people assembled for the celebration at the island city of Meroe and according to their traditions demanded human sacrifice of foreign captives of war. The prisoners now underwent the test of chastity by ascending the altar of fire and of course Theagenes and Chariclea passed the test.

The Gymnosophists through their leader Sisimithres refused to witness human sacrifice and foretold that this one would never be consummated. Chariclea begged them to stay and hear her case. (She had recognized Sisimithres' name as that of the one who had given her to Charicles at Catadupa). Chariclea declared that she was, a native, not a foreigner, and produced her fillet and her jewels among them the mystic ring, Pantarbé. Sisimithres narrated his part in her story. Hydaspes was puzzled over how he could have a *white* child, but Sisimithres explained that Persinna at the time of conception had fixed her eyes on a picture of the naked, white Andromeda. When the picture was brought in as evidence, Chariclea's resemblance to its Andromeda was found startling. Moreover a birthmark of a black ring around Chariclea's arm attested her black blood.

The people now refused to have Chariclea sacrificed, but the fate of Theagenes still hung in the balance. Chariclea begged that if he were to be sacrificed, she might perform the deed. (Apparently she planned to carry out a kind of suicide pact.) Hydaspes thought his daughter was insane and sent her into a tent with her mother while he received ambassadors and their gifts of victory. His nephew Meroebus brought a mighty athlete. Hydaspes as a joke gave him in return an elephant, but also promised him the hand of Chariclea. The Axiomitae presented a giraffe, an animal so strange that it terrified some of the natives. Moreover, one bull and two horses broke their fetters and dashed madly around the inside of the circle of guards. Theagenes mounted another horse, pursued the bull, wore it out and finally downed it. The enchanted spectators now demanded that he be matched with the champion Meroebus. Him too he vanquished. Oroondates crowned Theagenes as victor, but nevertheless prepared to sacrifice him.

At that moment ambassadors from Syene arrived with a letter from Oroondates. He begged that a young woman captive be sent to him with her father who was one of the ambassadors. This was Charicles. He recognized Theagenes and accused him of having stolen his daughter at Delphi. Theagenes revealed that Chariclea was the one demanded. Sisimithres told the rest of the story. Chariclea rushing out of the tent begged Charicles to forgive her elopement. Persinna told Hydaspes that she had learned that Chariclea was betrothed to Theagenes.

Sisimithres speaking not in Greek but in Ethiopian for all the people to hear ordered Hydaspes to submit to the will of the gods who had saved the two young lovers and who did not approve of human sacrifice and exhorted him to end human sacrifices forever. So Hydaspes asked the people to observe the will of the gods and to sanction the marriage of Theagenes and Chariclea. This they did. Then Hydaspes consecrated the two as priest and priestess of the Sun and the Moon and on their heads he placed the mitres which he and Persinna had worn as symbols of their offices. Thus was fulfilled the oracle :

> "In regions torrid shall arrive at last ;
> There shall the gods reward their pious vows,
> And snowy chaplets bind their dusky brows."

Then a great procession escorted them to Meroe there to fulfill the more mystic parts of wedlock.

In this brief re-telling of Heliodorus' long story, certain striking features of his structure appear. Geography and ethnography are important as in the other novelists. The eastern basin of the Mediterranean is the center of the adventures, the district which for centuries was the scene of the conflict for power between many nations. As in Xenophon, many geographical details are given, often with little accuracy.[7] As Maillon points out, imagination and

[7] Calderini, *op. cit.*, pp. 118-25.

fantasy falsify the historical and geographical allusions.
Heliodorus gathers everything that can satisfy the taste
for the strange and the marvellous. At a time when the
critical spirit was so little developed in the historians, a
writer of romance would naturally produce marvellous
narratives and vague descriptions. Heliodorus confuses
the Ethiopia of Herodotus with that of the Ptolemies and
imagines an Ethiopian empire which did not exist during
the domination of Egypt by the Persians.[8] As in Chariton, the superiority of the Greeks over the barbarians is
part of the author's faith.

In the development of the plot Heliodorus makes his
set more unified, less cinematic than Xenophon had done.
The scene of action lies almost entirely in Egypt with a
shift to Ethiopia for the final climax. This Egyptian set
is to be sure varied by different local scenes : the Nile,
an island village in its delta, towns such as Chemmis,
Memphis, Syene and Philae, the battle-fields of Bessa and
Elephantine, but nearly the whole plot develops in Egypt.
The exceptions are in the sub-plot presented in Cnemon's
narrative of his life-history which is laid in Athens, and
in Calasiris' long account of his visit to Delphi. These
however are clearly set off as insets in the unity of the
Egyptian scene.

The plot itself is an original combination of epic and
dramatic structure. The other writers of Greek romance
begin at the beginning with a detailed account of the hero
and heroine, their family, their background. Heliodorus
in true epic style plunges us *in medias res* with his startling
opening scene of a seascape where a ship rides at anchor,
treasure-laden but not manned, where the shore is littered
with the remains of a banquet, but strewn with corpses,
where a young man lies wounded with a beautiful maiden

---

[8] R. M. Rattenbury, T. W. Lumb, J. Maillon, *op. cit.*, I, lxxxviii–ix.

dressed as a goddess ministering to him. The reader is as amazed and puzzled at the sight as are the pirates who are peering down from the hills.

Another epic part of the structure is that the narrative of events does not proceed in a straight line but zigzags back and forth while a new arrival contributes his part to the development of the plot, or the author himself gives a retrospective résumé of past events to explain the present. Calasiris' long narrative is the best illustration of this resumptive method but Cnemon, Achaemenes, Sisimithres and Charicles all contribute their share of résumés.[9] In general, Heliodorus uses résumés with great effect to clarify his complicated plot. Sometimes he merely suggests a summary of events (V. 16, 5) ; sometimes he gives a full succinct recapitulation of events (II. 14, 1–2) ; sometimes his heroes recount their adventures to complain of them (V. 11).[10]

Many episodes too are taken from Homer. The games in Delphi in honor of Apollo are indebted to those given by Achilles in honor of Patroclus. The τειχοσκοπία where Arsace on the wall of Memphis watches the combat in the plain recalls Helen on the walls of Troy. The duel there between Thyamis and Theagenes is like one of the Homeric single combats. In it Theagenes' pursuit of Thyamis around the walls owes something to the pursuit of Hector by the swift-footed Achilles. The scar of Theagenes which is to be a sign of recognition was surely suggested by Odysseus'. The scene where the old woman evokes her dead son on the field of battle imitates the Homeric Νέκυια.[11]

---

[9] Calasiris in II and III ; Cnemon in I, II and VI ; Achaemenes in VIII ; Sisimithres and Charicles in X.

[10] R. M. Rattenbury, T. W. Lumb, J. Maillon, *op. cit.*, II, 87, n. 1.

[11] IV. 3, *Il.* XXII. 108–897 ; VII. 4–6, *Il.* III. 88–244 and *Il.* XXII. 136–436 ; V. 5, *Odys.* XIX. 392–94 ; VI. 14, *Odys.* XI.

Even more prominent than his debt to epic poetry is Heliodorus' use of dramatic structure. All the usual devices of Greek tragedy appear. Indeed the plot centers on the recognition of the young Greek heroine as the white Ethiopian princess by the tokens exposed with her in babyhood : her jewels, her mystic ring, her lettered fillet. This dramatic device of an agnorisis or recognition is multiplied by Heliodorus for repeated situations : the recognition of Chariclea in beggar's rags by Theagenes through her watchword, the identification of Charicles as her fosterfather and of Sisimithres as the noble Greek who found and saved the exposed child.

No less important is the usual Greek peripeteia, or reversal of fortune, for hero and heroine are repeatedly reunited only to be separated anew ; together or separately they are rescued from one catastrophe only to be plunged into a worse danger. Calasiris' long narrative resembles not only the ministrel's songs at the court of Alcinous of old far-off divine events, but also the messenger's speeches in tragedy wherein events too horrible or too complicated to be presented on the stage are told with a realism which starts the imagination. The mechanism of a parallel subplot is employed in Cnemon's life-story. The letter in Thisbe's dead hand is indebted to Phaedra's in Euripides' *Hippolytus*. Cybele, Arsace's maid, owes much in her character of confidant to Phaedra's nurse though she is more cynical and familiar. The crowd takes the place of the chorus, now demanding human sacrifice in the name of tradition, now releasing Chariclea from it through pity, now approving of the appeal of the noble Gymnosophists in the name of the gods to abolish the immolation of human victims. The *deus ex machina* is supplied by these very gods of the Gymnosophists, Helios, the Sun, and Se-

lene, the Moon, celestial symbols of pure deities of space
and time conceived in the philosophical mind.

Against this structure of drama the characters move as
though on a stage and even through the stylized formulae
of dramatic conventions usually attain individuality and
vitality. Maillon seems to me undiscriminating when he
speaks of them all as general types, not individuals, as
marionettes who can talk, lament and complain, but are
without life.[12] Even characters that fall into general
groups may as in real life have distinguishing traits and
in the list of characters certain are unforgettable person-
alities.

The hero Theagenes is of course supremely handsome
and physically strong. He is also as Wolff says spectacu-
larly courageous but easily discouraged.[13] He has to be
kept from suicide by Cnemon. He has to be cheered by
Chariclea. And his Lady Fair is the resourceful partner
in emergencies who whispers to him "Call me your Sister"
or invents means of recognition in case of separation or
makes a plot to share with him his fate be it life or death.
She demands too when they start off on travels together
that her lover swear a sacred oath to respect her virginity.
Indeed her leadership deserves the tribute given Dido,
dux femina facti. As Calderini notes, cleverness and deception were valued traits in those times and both she displayed.[14] But she guarded her chastity even from her
dearest and her courage never failed. On the battle field
she can shoot her arrows. She is surrounded by a divine
aura of radiant beauty that illuminates her holy garb.

The real hero of the romance is her father, the Ethiopian
King Hydaspes, whose qualities she seemed to have inherited. He is the type of the good king, but beyond that

[12] R. M. Rattenbury, T. W. Lumb,
J. Maillon, *op. cit.*, I, lxxxix–xcii.
[13] S. L. Wolff, *The Greek Romances*
in Elizabethan Prose Fiction, New
York, 1912, pp. 150–52.
[14] Calderini, *op. cit.*, pp. 106–7.

he is very human. He has his humor so that when his nephew presents him with a gigantic athletic champion he smilingly gives him in exchange an elephant. He is generous to a defeated foe, freeing Oroondates and restoring him to his office so that the viceroy makes obeisance to him and calls him the most just of mortals. He follows tradition in preparing to offer to the gods foreign captives as human victims, but when convinced by the Gymnosophists of the inappropriateness of such sacrifice he leads his people to the right decision about abolishing it and happily crowns his daughter and her lover as new priests of a purified worship.

Persinna his queen is a type of frustrated motherhood, timid enough to expose at birth her beautiful white baby for fear of the charge of adultery, but when her daughter is restored to her she glows with ardent parentalism and interprets Chariclea's wishes to her husband.

The characters in the sub-plot (Cnemon's story) are less clearly delineated than those in the main narrative. The story serves however not merely to introduce Thisbe, who is useful for the main plot, but anticipates and prepares for certain main characters. Aristippus the betrayed husband, Demaeneta the wanton wife, Thisbe the corrupt maid and Cnemon the coveted youth parallel Oroondates, Arsace, Cybele and Theagenes himself.

The far east opens up before us under the shadow of the Great King of the Persians. He never appears, but his viceroys, their lieutenants, their eunuchs work his will with the complete subservience which their act of obeisance symbolizes. Oroondates is a good fighter, but he is ready to desert secretly the city of Syene, which he has been defending, before terms of surrender had been concluded, to start another war in the name of the Great King. His will conveyed by letters must be law to his eunuch or his wife. This arbitrariness when imitated by his eunuch Euphrates becomes sadistic tyranny over prisoners given to his care.

Arsace his wife finds her escape in intrigue and amours.[15] Highly over-sexed she stops at nothing to satisfy her passion as her wanton fancies shift from one desired lover to another. She has no mercy for Theagenes when he is obdurate or for Chariclea when she finds she is the object of Theagenes' affections.

Cybele her maid abets her machinations and her lust. Though her position as confidante recalls Phaedra's nurse in the *Hippolytus,* her character reproduces all the venality, cunning and complaisance of the maids in new Attic comedy. Torture and murder are natural tools for success in her eyes and when she is hoist with her own petard, she dies asserting that she has been poisoned by the innocent girl whom she had hoped to make her victim. Arsace with her Cybele is a complete foil for the purity and loyalty of Chariclea.

The most interesting among the upright characters in the play are the priests : Calasiris, high-priest of Isis in Egypt, Charicles, priest of Apollo at Delphi, Sisimithres, the Greek Gymnosophist. They are consecrated to service, devoted to worship. They are men of the world extending their knowledge by travel and talk. Calasiris on his visit to Delphi spent his days in philosophical discussion of religious rites and the meaning of the gods of Greece and of Egypt. Charicles is a humanitarian who educates the little waif Chariclea as his own daughter. Sisimithres

---

[15] Arsace is not an historical character.

"Le personnage féminin d'Arsacé semble bien être de l'invention d'Héliodore, mais il se peut qu'il se soit souvenu, en créant son nom, d'Arsacés, le fondateur de l'empire des Parthes, et des Arsacides, ainsi que d'Arsamés, grandpère de Darius (Hér. I, 209). D'après Suidas (s.d. Θεοκλυτήσαντες) Darius avait une fille nommée Arsamé."

R. M. Rattenbury, T. W. Lumb, J. Maillon, *op. cit.*, **II, 113, n. 1.**

dares withdraw from the human sacrifices proposed by a great king and people and by his personal authority converts them from such abominable customs to a purer conception of deity and of worship. Calasiris in his role of interpreting the events of the story and solving its problems, in his clear philosophical interests probably represents Heliodorus himself.[16]

To return to the structure of the romance, the plot with such borrowings from epic and dramatic poetry, with such characters, some types, some highly individualized, moves forward in a manner that resembles the modern cinema. There is no carefully interwoven plot such as tragedy presents, for example in *Oedipus Rex*. Rather there is a progression of episodes, each a clear picture in itself, all after many involutions and evolutions falling into an orderly narrative. Rattenbury thinks that after Heliodorus' original beginning which secures the interest and sympathy of the reader through his curiosity he fails to maintain the interest throughout. The long retrospective narrative of Calasiris becomes monotonous. The reader is irritated by the postponement of the denouement after he as well as the hero and heroine knows the secret of Chariclea's parentage. Maillon, however, finds in Heliodorus a great talent for narration. After the impressive opening scene, he says, from narrative to narrative, from description to description, one is led slowly but without ennui to the grandeur of the final chapters. The variety of the episodes does not detract from the unity of the narrative because we keep returning to Theagenes and Chariclea in whom we have been interested from the first.[17]

To me personally the defects in the romance lie not in the long narrative of Calasiris or in the early revelation of

[16] R. M. Rattenbury, T. W. Lumb, J. Maillon, *op. cit.*, I, lxxxv–viii.

[17] R. M. Rattenbury, T. W. Lumb, J. Maillon, *op. cit.*, I, xviii–xx.

Chariclea's identity, but in the excessive use of descriptive passages. Planned though they undoubtedly are to satisfy the craving of the age for a knowledge of the novel and the strange, or to give local color, they retard the development of the story. Often they are prolix and difficult because of an unfamiliar vocabulary and a complicated sentence structure. There are many such passages : descriptions of natural phenomena (the island city in the delta of the Nile, the straits at Calydon) ; of curious animals (crocodile and giraffe) ; of operations of war (a naval battle, the siege of Syene, the duel of Thyamis and Petosiris) ; the religious ceremonies at Delphi. These vary greatly in clarity and effectiveness, but in general they tend to be verbose and to retard the narrative. Such descriptions are however one of the conventional features of the Greek romance. And with all Heliodorus' originality in plot, in his tripartite structure of epic, dramatic and cinematic features, he employs all the usual devices of Greek romance. These are oracle and oath, résumés, conversation and rhetorical speeches, letters and soliloquies, meditated suicide and apparent death, dreams and epiphanies. But Heliodorus makes these conventional devices integral parts of his plot.

The oracle given by the Pythian priestess at Delphi early in the story motivates the plot until the very end when its meaning is explained and its prophecy fulfilled. . The oath which Chariclea requires of her lover early in her travels protects her chastity through all the intimacies of palace apartment and prison dungeons. Résumés of events given several times by Cnemon, by Calasiris in his long narrative, by Charicles, clarify and facilitate the plot.[18] Conversation is used constantly on the battle field or in the

[18] "Héliodore pratique avec une réelle habileté l'art des suspensions et des retours. L'unité du récit n'est jamais compromise."
R. M. Rattenbury, T. W. Lumb, J. Maillon, *op. cit.*, II, 37, n. 3.

boudoir, in palaces, in dungeons. Turn over the pages of Heliodorus' Greek as you would a modern novel and test how often the pages are broken and enlivened by talk. Rhetoric colors some of the longer speeches, but in the court-room scene (the trial of Chariclea for poisoning Cybele) the procedure is described but the speeches are not quoted.

Letters are as important as oracles for the development of the plot. The letter of Persinna inscribed on the fillet exposed with her child furnishes the indisputable evidence for the recognition of Chariclea. The letter in Thisbe's dead hand is of prime importance in the sub-plot in announcing to Cnemon the death of his wicked step-mother. Business letters of Mithranes to Oroondates, of Oroondates to Arsace and to the eunuch Euphrates, of Hydaspes to the Supreme Council of Ethiopia and to his queen Persinna furnish documentation for the march of events. The letter of Oroondates to Hydaspes in the last book prepares the way for Charicles' final explanation of his relation to his foster-daughter and his own recognition of Chariclea.

Soliloquies reveal emotional states and meditated suicide. At Chemmis one night Chariclea left alone yields to despair and vows that if she learns Theagenes is dead, she will join him in the shades. An apparent death nearly precipitates tragedy when in the dark of the cave the body of Thisbe is mistaken for that of Chariclea. Theagenes bursts into despairing lamentation and proposes suicide. But Cnemon foreseeing this has filched his sword and presently the light of Cnemon's torch reveals the truth and there ensues a happy reversal of fortune.

Among all these usual features of the plot a new importance is given to dreams and epiphanies. They are peculiarly significant because of their bearing on Heli-

odorus' philosophical and religious interests. Some motivate minor events or simply create atmosphere. Thyamis
in the night before the battle with another band of brigands had a vision of Isis who gave Chariclea to him with
the mystic words : "Having her, you will not have her,
but you will be unjust and will kill the stranger. And
she will not be killed." At first Thyamis, interpreting
the dream in accordance with his own wishes, thought it
meant that he would murder her virginity, but she would
live. Then when the battle went against him, he changed
his interpretation and to save Chariclea from his foes,
killed her (as he thought) in the cave. So Thisbe's death
is explained. Another dream of little importance is Chariclea's in which a wild looking man appeared and pierced
her right eye with his sword. Opposing interpretations
are given by Theagenes and Cnemon. The epiphanies,
however, which are vitally significant for the plot all foretell the final fortunes of the hero and the heroine. To
Calasiris Apollo and Diana appeared, the god leading
Theagenes, the goddess Chariclea, and intrusted them
to him. Diana too bade him consider the pair as his
children and take them to Egypt when and how the gods
should decree. Charicles too dreamed that an eagle flew
from the hand of Apollo, seized Chariclea and bore her
away from Delphi to a land of dark forms. Calasiris again
had a vision, this time of Odysseus, the great traveller, who
demanded sacrifices and presented Penelope's blessing on
Chariclea. Calasiris after his death himself appeared
simultaneously to Chariclea and Theagenes, telling the
heroine that the Pantarbè jewel would protect her, and
telling the hero that he would be freed from Arsace and
take his Lady to Ethiopia. Hydaspes, when the prisoner
Chariclea is brought before him, recalled a dream that a
full-grown daughter was born to him and the face of this

dream-girl was Chariclea's. This prepared him for the real recognition of her identity. Now the validity of these apparitions is sometimes questioned : are they dreams or visions ? The author comments that desire often prompts favorable interpretation. He has Hydaspes' officers tell him that the mind creates for itself fantasies which seem to foretell future events. He has the optimistic Chariclea encourage Theagenes to trust in the gods and interpret Calasiris' prophecies as beneficent. But all the same Heliodorus motivates his plot by this popular belief in dreams and epiphanies.

This structural element fits in with the religious-philosophical coloring of the whole background. Dreams and epiphanies, miracles and necromancy are partial manifestations of a deep-seated interest in cults and philosophies that is a phenomenon of the times. There is a long description of the festival of Neoptolemus at Delphi with its pageantry, sacrifices, hymn, dance, libations and the lighting of the pyre. It is here that Theagenes and Chariclea meet and at first sight fall in love. Nausicles the merchant must sacrifice to Hermes, god of trade. The festival of the overflowing of the Nile is celebrated in Egypt. And among the Ethiopians the first fruits of victory in war are offered in the form of sacrifice of human captives to their gods. The most prominent cults are those of Apollo-Helios of Delphi, Egypt and Ethiopia and of the Egyptian Isis. These are savior gods to whom mortals offer petitions for salvation.

Opinions differ as to whether the representation of the cult of Helios is the usual conventional religious background of a Greek romance or whether it is the author's glorification of the cult of his native city with which he and his family had some official connection. At the antipodes in criticism are Rattenbury who perceives only the usual religious conventions and Calderini who thinks the unique feature of the *Aethiopica* is its rich philosophical coloring.[19] All would agree on marked influence in Heliodorus of Neo-Pythagoreanism and the teachings of Apollonius of Tyana as recorded by Philostratus.[20] Maillon in his preface gives this discriminating summary of his own position towards Heliodorus' philosophical interests. He says that the Pantheon of Heliodorus does not contain many deities. He refers to the gods under the Neo-Pythagorean name of οἱ κρείττονες. Calasiris whose role is most important may well represent the author's state of mind. This priest of Isis practices a large eclecticism. He goes to Delphi and divides his time between the service of the temple and theological discussion. He worships especially one god, Apollo of Delphi, Helios of Emesa. Apollo directs the drama of his story, Helios crowns it in Ethiopia. One sees in Heliodorus the intention of simplifying and unifying mythology and of bringing back religion to its eastern and Egyptian origins. Instead of wishing to discredit pagan stories, he treats them philosophically to make them acceptable to an age which was becoming emancipated and more severe and to a new faith which wished to reconcile the philosophical tradition and the sense of the divine and the mysterious.

Neo-Pythagoreanism was a curious attempt to found a religion which would satisfy both the critical spirit and the people. At the beginning of the third century appeared *The Life of Apollonius of Tyana,* a magician and a disciple of Pythagoras. Philostratus takes his hero to the Orient, Ethiopia, Greece, Rome. He writes a real

[19] R. M. Rattenbury, T. W. Lumb, J. Maillon, *op. cit.,* I, xx–xxi and lxxxv–viii ; A. Calderini, *op. cit.,* pp. 176–77.
[20] See *The Cambridge Ancient History,* Cambridge (Eng.), 1934, X, 506–11 ; 1936, XI, 700–1 ; Philostratus, *The Life of Apollonius of Tyana* translated by F. C. Conybeare in *The Loeb Classical Library,* 2 vols. New York, 1912.

romance. And that of Heliodorus recalls it often. Both authors show the same admiration for the Gymnosophists, the same distinction between magic and theurgy. Both Apollonius and Calasiris are opposed to impure sacrifices. The story of the magical Pantarbè jewel appears in both Philostratus and Heliodorus. Calasiris like Apollonius is a model of Pythagorean asceticism. Apollonius defends himself about working miracles and lets a doubt appear about his theurgic powers. Calasiris shows in daily life a common wisdom and reserves for exceptional cases an appeal to great demons.

In the *Aethiopica* dreams play a more important role than the demons. Communications with the invisible world are constant, but only exceptional human beings who have had long experience in divine matters and a life mortified and purified by expiation know the mysteries of the invisible world.

This paraphrase of Maillon's paragraphs shows how completely logical is the conclusion of the romance where the noble Gymnosophist Sisimithres persuades the king of the Ethiopians and his people to renounce human sacrifice and accept the divine blessing on the loves of Theagenes and Chariclea.

"At length Hydaspes said to Sisimithres, 'O sage ! What are we to do ? To defraud the gods of their victims is not pious ; to sacrifice those who appear to be preserved and restored by their providence is impious. It needs that some expedient be found out.'

Sisimithres, speaking, not in the Grecian, but in the Ethiopian tongue, so as to be heard by the greatest part of the assembly, replied : 'O king ! The wisest among men, as it appears, often have the understanding clouded through excess of joy, else, before this time, you would have discovered that the gods regard not with favour the sacrifice which you have been preparing for them. First they, from the very altar, declared the all-blessed Chariclea to be your daughter ; next they brought her foster-father most wonderfully from the midst of Greece to this spot ; they struck panic and terror into the horses and oxen which were being prepared for sacrifice, indicating, perhaps, by that event, that those whom custom considered as the more perfect and fitting victims were to be rejected. Now, as the consummation of all good, as the perfection of the piece, they show this Grecian youth to be the betrothed husband of the maiden. Let us give credence to these proofs of the divine and wonder-working will ; let us be fellow workers with this will ; let us have recourse to holier offerings ; let us abolish, for ever, these detested human sacrifices.' " [21]

A few words must be said on the style of Heliodorus. It is predominantly literary, but extremely varied. He uses Homer almost as much as Chariton does. His adaptation of Homeric episodes has already been described.[22] A discussion of Homer and his parentage between Calasiris and Cnemon is introduced in the style of the rhetorical schools.[23] Descriptions as well as episodes owe much to Homeric coloring, witness the epiphany of Odysseus.[24] But above all the language itself is almost as rich in quotations from Homer as is Chariton's.

Often reminiscent phraseology betrays quotations in solution. Frequently too very famous phrases are quoted directly. Calasiris greets Nausicles with that best of all wishes : "May the gods give you your heart's desire !" Nausicles reminds Calasiris that the gifts of the gods are not to be despised. The maid Cybele assures Arsace that soon Theagenes will desert Chariclea for her, exchanging bronze for gold.[25] Emotional crises are described or expressed in Homer's words. Arsace's sleeplessness has the same manifestations as Achilles. Cnemon upbraids Chariclea for her pessimism about Theagenes' fate in the words of Agamemnon to Chalchas. And Chariclea when she is questioned by physicians as to the cause of her illness only keeps repeating : "Achilles, Peleus' son, noblest of

[21] Translated by the Rev. Rowland Smith, *op. cit.*, p. 259.
[22] p. 78.
[23] III. 12–15.

[24] V. 22, *Odys.* XIII. 332, XVIII. 66–70, *Il.* XIX. 47–49.
[25] V. 11, *Odys.* VI. 180 ; V. 15, *Il.* III. 65 ; VII. 10, *Il.* VI. 235–36.

Greeks !" as though only the apostrophe uttered by Patroclus could describe her dear Theagenes.[26]   These are but
a few illustrations of Heliodorus' constant use of Homeric
diction.

No less did he use the language of the theater.[27]   We
have already seen how much his plot owes to the structure
of Greek tragedy.   From drama he took also a vocabulary
of pungent metaphors to describe the progress of events
in his story.   Repeatedly the action is referred to as a
tragedy.[28]   And certain scenes by their wording imply a
recognition, a *deus ex machina,* a prologue and a change
from tragedy to comedy.   These may, as Calderini suggests, be reminiscences of contemporary plays now lost,
which readers of the time would recognize.[29]   Certainly
structure and language of the romance attest Heliodorus'
deep interest in the theater.

The third striking element in the diction of Heliodorus
is the rhetorical.   He often uses all the artifices taught
in the schools : alliterations, antitheses, set phrases.   He
loves the grand style.   A speech, even one uttered by his
charming heroine, is an opportunity for pomposity.   He
uses in excess that fine writing for descriptive passages
which the schools taught and he scatters throughout his
narrative pithy truisms or *sententiae* which were part of
the capital of the rhetorician.

But these lapses into over-refined phrases, laborious
symmetry and decorative rhetoric are less of a barrier to
a modern reader than is his syntax.   His sentence structure in general is not paratactic as is so much of Chariton

---

[26] VII. 9, *Il.* XXIV. 3–12 ; VI. 5,
Il. I. 106–7 ; IV. 7, *Il.* XVI. 21.
[27] J. W. H. Walden, *Stage-terms
in Heliodorus's Aethiopica,* in "Harvard Studies in Classical Philology,"
V (1894), 1–43.

[28] V. 6, II. 11, I. 3, II. 4 and 23,
VI. 12, IX. 5, VI. 14.
[29] X. 12, VII. 6–8, VIII. 17. Calderini, *op. cit.,* pp. 159–63.

and of Xenophon, but complex. Moreover these complex sentences are often exceedingly long with a kind of agglutinative accumulation of participial constructions that demands re-reading for comprehension. Yet he can be simple and pellucid in rapid narrative and emotional crises as the final Book shows. And it is just because much of his narrative is so exciting that we fall into resentful criticism when Homer nods in dull drowsiness.[30]

Although we cannot date the *Aethiopica* more exactly than somewhere in the third century (probably in the first half), the romance reflects in general the life of the times in which Heliodorus lived. The east daubs its brilliant colors upon the story as the power of oriental rulers impinges on the life of the Greeks. The absolutism of the Great King of Persia is the model for minor courts of viceroys and their queens who demand of their subjects and captives the obeisance that they must render to their Super-Ruler. Military officers and eunuchs are the descending steps in this hierarchy of tyranny.

Adventures center in war and travel. Cities and tribes revolt. Heroes must display military virtues. Merchants, priests and women travel widely, braving the dangers of storms at sea and of attacks by pirates. Women have found a new freedom and are leaders in courage and endurance as the story of Chariclea shows. Women take part in banquets and religious ceremonies as well as in adventures. Romantic friendship between men and admiration of young men's beauty are a counterpart of the famous relation between Hadrian and Antinous. Slaves and captives may become court favorites or be subjected to indignities, imprisonment, torture.

[30] On the style of Heliodorus, see Maillon in R. M. Rattenbury, T. W. Lumb, J. Maillon, *op. cit.*, I, xcii–xciii.

The times are characterized too by an eager search for the new, the unfamiliar, by scientific curiosity, by an interest in art.. So descriptions of strange countries and peoples, accounts of strange adventures and sights are part of the novelist's stock in trade. He describes vividly the island city in the Nile's delta, its water-ways through the reeds, its cave refuge with its secret entrance ; or he gives a technical account of the engineering processes by which a city is besieged by threat of inundation ; or he pictures such a curiosity in the animal world as a giraffe. Works of art are featured with admiring care : Theagenes' embroidered robe and its clasp, Chariclea's robe and its girdle, the amethyst ring with its carved scene, the painting of Perseus and Andromeda, nude, shining, chained to the rock.

And part of the picture of the times centers in man's quest for new values for life itself. Ethical standards for conduct are weighed and emphasized in contrasts between Greeks and barbarians. Aspiration towards the higher life is portrayed in the worship of the gods and its ceremonials and in the philosophical discussions in which the priests take part. The Gymnosophists and Calasiris share a large humanity.

The primary interests of the romance, however, far outweighing its philosophy and its adventures, is love. Once more two enchanting young people meet at a festival of a god, fall in love at first sight, plight their troth, accompany each other through world-wide adventures, preserve their faith and their chastity and for their piety are at last united in perfect happiness. Theagenes and Chariclea join Chaereas and Callirhoe, Habrocomes and Anthia, Clitophon and Leucippe, Daphnis and Chloe in the undying annals of true love. And the reader closes Heliodorus' novel with Cnemon's comment :

> "I am at feud with Homer, father, for saying that love, as well
> as everything else, brings satiety in the end ; for my part I am
> never tired either of feeling it myself, or hearing of its influence on
> others ; and lives there the man of so iron and adamantine an
> heart, as not to be enchanted with listening to the loves of Theag-
> enes and Chariclea, though the story were to last a year ?" [31]

[31] IV. 4.   Translated by the Rev. Rowland Smith, *op. cit.*, p. 81.

V

THE ADVENTURES OF LEUCIPPE AND CLITOPHON

BY ACHILLES TATIUS

"EVERY ROMANCE," says Aristide Calderini in writing of the Greek novels, "represents successively a new advance or a new type in its genre. Now the closest affiliation is with history, now with pastoral poetry, now with philosophy. While certain common elements persist, the general pattern of the whole changes ; often the content is varied ; often the limits." [1]

The variation within this new form of literature is richly illustrated by the novel we are now to study, the one which was probably written last of the extant Greek Romances as Chariton's was the first. This is *The Adventures of Leucippe and Clitophon* of Achilles Tatius.

We know little of the author. Suidas, the lexicographer of the tenth century, wrote his brief biography :

"Achilles Statius" (note the incorrect form of the name 'Tatius') "of Alexandria : the writer of the story of Leucippe and Clitophon, as well as other episodes of love, in eight books. He finally became a Christian and a bishop. He also wrote a treatise on the sphere, and works on etymology, and a mixed narration telling of many great and marvellous men. His novel is in all respects like that of the other writers of love-romances." [2]

---

[1] Aristide Calderini, *Caritone di Afrodisia, Le Avventure di Cherea e Calliroe*, Torino, 1913, p. 191.

[2] From the introduction to *Achilles Tatius* with an English translation by S. Gaselee, in *The Loeb Classical Library*. The translations used in this chapter are from this volume.

Now though Suidas used earlier material and essayed accuracy, two statements in this biography are manifestly incorrect. There is nothing whatever in the romance to indicate that Tatius was ever a Christian and the story about his conversion and bishopric probably duplicates the similar tradition about his predecessor, Heliodorus, who was identified with a bishop of Tricca who bore his name. Moreover Tatius' novel is very different in many particulars from all the romances which are now known. And it is these contrasts rather than the similarities which make him in our studies so excellent a foil for Chariton.

The date of about A.D. 300 is probably right for the novel because the author seems to imitate the style of certain romancers of the third century and because a recently discovered papyrus fragment [3] shows that for palaeographical reasons this earliest manuscript could not have been written later than the first half of the fourth century. This evidence about the lateness of Achilles Tatius we shall find borne out by a deterioration in style from Chariton's simplicity to an over-elaboration and exaggeration and a change in spirit from sincerity to ironic parody.[4]

One important reason for knowing Achilles Tatius is "his contributions to Elizabethan prose fiction and, through this, to the making of the modern novel." [5] The first Greek text was not published until 1601 but before this he was made known to the sixteenth century by translations in Latin, Italian and French. And in 1597 the first English translation, that of William Burton, appeared. Todd succinctly states his resulting influence :

"With Heliodorus, though in less measure, he furnished structure and material for Sidney's *Arcadia,* and thus was among the

[3] GH in Grenfell and Hunt, *Oxyrhynchus Papyri,* X, 135, no. 1250.
[4] R. T. Rattenbury, *New Chapters in the History of Greek Literature :*

Third Series: Oxford, 1933, pp. 254–57.
[5] F. A. Todd, *Some Ancient Novels,* Oxford, 1940, p. 33 ; S. Gaselee, *op. cit.,* pp. xv–xvi.

influences that formed the novels of Richardson and Walter Scott ; of Greene, as Dr. S. L. Wolff puts it, he was the 'first and latest love' ; in Lyly himself, and not only in him, we recognize Tatius as one of the sources of English Euphuism." [6]

My plan in taking up Achilles Tatius is first to analyze briefly his plot and then summarize its similarities to *Chaereas and Callirhoe* and the other Greek novels.　Then I shall discuss more in detail the unique features in Tatius and his special characteristics.

An epigram in the Palatine Anthology, attributed to Photius, patriarch of Constantinople, but by some to Leon the philosopher gives a bird's eye view of the story.[7]

"The story of Clitophon reveals to the eyes, as it were, a bitter love but a virtuous life.　The very virtuous life of Leucippe puts all in ecstasy, (for the story tells) how she was beaten and shorn of her hair and clothed pitiably, and — the greatest point — having died three times she endured to the end.　And if you too wish to be virtuous, friend, do not consider the side issues of the plot, but learn first the outcome of the story, for it joins in marriage those who love sanely."

For the expansion of this epitome it is necessary to have before us a list of the many characters in the romance.

Chief characters :

Clitophon, a Greek of Tyre, son of Hippias
Leucippe, daughter of Sostratus of Byzantium, the uncle of Clitophon
Clinias of Sidon, cousin of Clitophon
Chaereas of Pharos, a fisherman
Melitte, a woman of Ephesus
Thersander, the husband of Melitte
Callisthenes of Byzantium
Calligone, the half-sister of Clitophon

Minor characters :

Sostratus, of Byzantium, father of Leucippe
Panthea, his wife

---

[6] F. A. Todd, *op. cit.,* p. 33 ; S. L. Wolff, *The Greek Romances in Elizabethan Prose Fiction,* New York, 1912, pp. 248–56.
[7] Pal. Anth. IX. 203.

Hippias, a Tyrian, father of Clitophon and Calligone
Charicles, the *amicus* of Clinias
Menelaus, an Egyptian
Sosthenes, the bailiff of Thersander
Satyrus, a slave of Clitophon
Clio, Leucippe's chambermaid, in love with Satyrus
Charmides, an Egyptian general
Gorgias, an Egyptian soldier

For the plot I condense Phillimore's well-written summary.[8] The author begins with a description of Sidon. He has reached Sidon in his travels and is touring the city, looking at the temples. He describes a painting of Zeus and Europa, also a statue of Eros. He was reflecting on the Eros : "Think of such a brat being lord of earth and sea !" When a young man near testifies to Eros' power which he has felt, the author invites him to tell his story. In a Platonic scene under a plane-tree near a stream they sit down.

The stranger, Clitophon, a Greek of Tyre, tells his story in the first person. Clitophon has been unwillingly betrothed at nineteen to his half-sister, Calligone. Now his uncle, Sostratus, writes that he is sending his daughter Leucippe and her mother from their home in Byzantium to Tyre for safety during a war. Clitophon at once falls in love with Leucippe. He makes his cousin, Clinias, his confidant. Clinias is sympathetic because he had a tragic love affair with a youth who was killed by a fall from a horse which Clinias gave him. (Here is introduced a purple patch on the driving accident.)

Encouraged by Clinias, Clitophon makes love constantly. Various scenes of his wooing, for example a garden, are described in detail. Finally the lovers elope, find a ship at Berytus, embark and start to Alexandria. They meet an Egyptian fellow-passenger, Menelaus.

[8] J. S. Phillimore, "The Greek Romances," in *English Literature and the Classics,* Oxford, 1912, pp. 108–15.

There comes a great storm. Hero and heroine are cast
on shore at Pelusium near the temple of Zeus Casius.
Enter black brigands. Soldiers rescue Clitophon, but
Leucippe is kidnapped. Clitophon joins in an attempt
to save her, but it is baulked by a deep, impassable canal
between the rescuing party and the ten thousand brigands. Across it Clitophon watches the bandits perform
a human sacrifice by disembowelling the victim before
an altar. It is Leucippe. The body is put in a coffin.

The next day the canal is diked and crossed. Clitophon
resolves to die on Leucippe's body, but suddenly he meets
his slave Satyrus and Menelaus, both saved from the wreck,
who assure him that Leucippe is alive. On the coffin
being opened, she comes out — "Gashed open and minus
all viscera." But the murderers had been deceived by a
sheepskin full of animal entrails attached to her and by
a stage sword which never penetrated her body. Clinias
too was saved from the wreck. Now a punitive expedition under Charmides, the Egyptian, starts, but unfortunately he falls in love with Leucippe and has a philtre
given her which drives her insane. On her recovery they
go to Alexandria. There a new rival, Chaereas, abducts
Leucippe. Clitophon pursues on a ship of war, but has
to endure seeing Leucippe beheaded on the deck of the
enemy's vessel. Clitophon recovers the head from the
sea and gives it burial.

Six months later Clitophon meets Clinias again. Clinias
who had been home in Sidon reports that "the cruel parent
had actually betrothed the loving cousins" so Clitophon
and Leucippe might have married in peace. Clitophon
who naturally believes Leucippe dead is pursued by Melitte, a lovely, wealthy and amorous widow of Ephesus.
He finally yields to her ; they are betrothed in the temple
of Isis and are to be married when they reach Ephesus.

On their arrival, Melitte drives Clitophon around her great estates. There he has the overwhelming surprise of encountering Leucippe who is working in the garden as a miserable slave. This difficult situation is made more complicated by the sudden reappearance of Melitte's husband, Thersander, who had been falsely reported drowned at sea. Thersander beats up Clitophon as an adulterer with his wife and has him imprisoned.

Sosthenes, the bailiff of Thersander, interests his master in Leucippe, so he tries to seduce her, but unsuccessfully. Clitophon in prison is told a false story that both Leucippe and Melitte are faithless to him. Clitophon resolves to denounce Melitte as an accomplice in a plot for the murder of Leucippe and then to die. He is tried for adultery and self-confessed murder, but Clinias foils his attempt by telling the whole truth in court. Sosthenes departs, leaving Leucippe free. Leucippe's father, Sostratus, by good fortune arrives in Ephesus on a sacred embassy just in time to assist his daughter. The trial of Clitophon is resumed in a long court scene in which finally Thersander challenges Leucippe and Melitte to tests of chastity by the magic pipes of Pan and the magic spring of Rhodopis. Both pass the ordeals. Thersander, since everything is going against him, for his slave, Sosthenes, has been captured and will be forced to confess the truth, flees. Sosthenes confesses. Clitophon is acquitted. Leucippe tells her whole story : how the bandits beheaded another woman dressed in her clothes to prevent Clitophon from following ; how a quarrel over her arose among them in which Chaereas was slain ; then she was sold by the other pirates to Sosthenes, who bought her for Thersander. Sostratus then relates the secondary romance of Callisthenes and Calligone. The novel ends with a happy reunion of all at Tyre where prayers and sacrifices are offered in behalf of the lasting felicity of Clitophon and Leucippe, of Callisthenes and Calligone.

Such is the story which Phillimore characterizes as "a breathless succession of improbable incident." [9] The settings move with the same cinematic rapidity which Chariton employed : from Sidon to Berytus, to the sea and shipwreck, to Pelusium and Alexandria, to Ephesus and the great court scene, to Byzantium and back again to Tyre.

In one point particularly the structure of the plot differs from Chariton's and indeed from the plots of all the other Greek Romances. The author in the beginning hands over the story to a narrator, the hero, Clitophon, who then tells the events in the first person. Very soon, however, the reader has forgotten this device : so many other characters are given the floor to relate their own tales. And at the end the author too has forgotten this beginning, for Clitophon does not round up his narrative with a polite farewell. He does not even explain how he happened to be at Sidon where he started the tale. And the author does not express his appreciation of the entertainment Clitophon has given him.[10]

The chief interests of the romance are again love, adventure and religion. There are two love-stories of primary interest instead of one. Yet the bulk of the plot turns on adventure rather than on sex or worship. And delight in adventure adds to the typical travellers' tales a flaming curiosity which demands description of many strange novelties.

In general the technical devices common to all the romances are used. There is much conversation. There

---

9 J. S. Phillimore, *op. cit.*, p. 115.   10 S. Gaselee, *op. cit.*, p. 455.

are many soliloquies. Clitophon upbraids himself for swerving from Calligone to Leucippe.[11] Later he bemoans Leucippe's fate when she has been kidnapped by the blacks.[12] Leucippe, sold as a slave, laments her whole sad love-story while lustful Thersander is eavesdropping outside the door.[13] Clitophon, on hearing in prison the false story that Leucippe has been murdered by Melitte, voices his horror over her death and over the fact that he had kissed her slayer.[14] These soliloquies are employed to reveal the intense feelings of hero and heroine at emotional crises.

Three letters are used. The first is a brief business letter which serves to develop the plot, for in it Sostratus writes to his brother Hippias that he is sending his daughter Leucippe and his wife Panthea to him for safe-keeping until the war between the Byzantines and the Thracians is over.[15] The other two are love-letters. One is Leucippe's to Clitophon telling him that she has been sold as a slave, begging for ransom money, wishing him happiness in his coming nuptials with Melitte, and assuring him she is still a virgin. The other is Clitophon's answer declaring that he has "imitated her virginity, if there be any virginity in men," begging her not to judge him until he can explain all, but to pity him.[16] Leucippe's letter is found by Melitte and helps motivate the plot in its emotional aspects, for it works Melitte up through jealousy and despair to such passionate ardor that she persuades Clitophon to sleep one night with her.[17]

Oaths are not important in the structure of the plot. Once Leucippe swears to her father by Artemis that she has told him a true story about being still a maid.[18]

11 II. 5.
12 III. 10.
13 VI. 16.
14 VII. 5.

15 I. 3.
16 V. 18–20.
17 V. 25–27.
18 VIII. 7.

Dreams are frequent and are significant. Four are reported which are vital factors in the plot. Clitophon's father dreams that while he is conducting the wedding ceremonies of his son and Calligone the torches are extinguished. This dream leads him to hasten the marriage so distasteful to Clitophon and it would have been consummated at once had not Calligone been kidnapped by Callisthenes under the impression that she was Leucippe.[19] Then Clitophon had persuaded Leucippe to let him spend the night with her and with the aid of Satyrus was already in her bedroom. Leucippe's mother who had just had a dream that a robber with a naked sword was playing the part of Jack the Ripper with her daughter, rushed in and interrupted the amour.[20] Later on, Leucippe and Clitophon on the same night have similar dreams. A goddess appears and warns each that their love must not be consummated until the goddess decks the bride and opens her temple to the bridegroom. This apparition makes them postpone the rites of Aphrodite.[21] In Book VII Sostratus, Leucippe's father, sees in a dream an apparition of Artemis who tells him that he will find Leucippe and Clitophon in Ephesus. He goes to Ephesus then on a sacred embassy and finds that Artemis does not lie.[22]

This tendency to a repeated use of the same device for forwarding the plot is seen in greater extravagance and exaggeration in the use of apparent deaths. Leucippe is supposed to meet violent death three times, twice before the eyes of her lover, once in vivid narrative told to him in prison. First she is sacrificed by brigands by being disembowelled before an altar. Second she is beheaded on the deck of a ship by black pirates and her head tossed into the ocean. Third she is murdered by an assassin

19 II. 11–17.
20 II. 23.
21 IV. 1.

22 VII. 12, 14. Compare also the dream in I. 3.

hired by Melitte.[23]   In the first two cases ghastly details
make the executions seem real, but Leucippe always sur-
vives and reappears with a plausible but exotic story.
Surely in this exaggeration Achilles Tatius is using thinly
veiled satire of the device of improbable reappearances in
the Greek romance.

The same exuberance appears in the use of the forensic
speeches, of long, mythological narratives and of wordy
descriptions.   All these will be considered in the study
of the style of the romance.   Two more technical devices
of the plot must be mentioned here : the use of résumés
and the usual happy ending.   Book VIII is crowded with
résumés : Clitophon tells all his adventures to Sostratus
and the priest of Artemis.   Leucippe relates to Sostratus
how the pirates decapitated another woman in her place.
Finally Sostratus relates to his daughter and to Clitophon
the romance of Callisthenes and Calligone.[24]   The romances of both pairs of lovers, Clitophon and Leucippe,
Callisthenes and Calligone, are concluded by happy weddings.   And among the leading characters only Melitte
suffers final disappointment.   Achilles Tatius ironically
grants her at least one memorable embrace on a prison
floor !

The character drawing is much less elaborate than the
plot.   While plot and counterplot of the two romances
interplay, the young hero Clitophon and the beautiful Leucippe are more or less conventional figures who
move glamorously, weeping, fainting, dreaming, voyaging, through preposterous adventures.   But Callisthenes,
the secondary hero, is far more interesting than Clitophon
because his character shows startling development.   And
Melitte, though she plays the part of temptress, is a great
human creation.

23 III. 15 ; V. 7 ; VII. 3–5.   24 VIII. 4–5, 15–17.

In Book II Callisthenes first appears as a wealthy orphan, who is notoriously dissipated and extravagant. Wishing to marry beauty and having a strange streak of romanticism he asked Sostratus for the hand of the beautiful Leucippe although he had never seen her. Rejected by Sostratus as a suitor because of his bad reputation he plotted vengeance in his willful and violent way. He journeyed to Tyre, saw Calligone at a festival, mistook her for Leucippe, fell in love at first sight, hired some gangsters to kidnap her and sailed off with his prize.[25] Callisthenes does not reappear until in the end of Book VIII Sostratus tells the story of his reform.[26] On the voyage Callisthenes found himself madly in love with Calligone, revealed to her that he was no pirate but a wealthy Byzantine noble, offered her honorable marriage and a large dowry, and promised to respect her chastity as long as she desired. At Byzantium, love transformed him so that he appeared courteous, virtuous, self-controlled. He showed great respect for his elders. He was no longer extravagant, but became philanthropic. He gave large contributions to the state. He trained for military service and won distinction in actual warfare. In this changed guise he secured Sostratus as an advocate to persuade Hippias to give him the hand of Calligone, whose chastity he had scrupulously respected. Eros thus salvaged Callisthenes and then rewarded him.

Melitte the widow of Ephesus is the most elaborately drawn character in the romance. There is even a long personal description of her : she is as beautiful as a statue with skin like milk, cheeks roses, hair thick, long, golden, and about her the radiance of Aphrodite. Clitophon admits he saw her with pleasure. Indeed she is so magnetic that the kisses she was pleased to bestow on him stirred him.[27] She knew what she wanted and how to get it.

[25] II. 13, 15–18.
[26] VIII. 17–18.
[27] V. 11, 13.

During four months she had to woo Clitophon though she was rich and young and her husband has been lost at sea. Finally since Clitophon was convinced that Leucippe was really dead, he yielded and agreed to marry her, though on condition that they should not be united until they arrived at Ephesus. She was as passionate as Clitophon was cold. On the ship she made ardent love to him while he begged her to philosophize on love's nature. After Clitophon secretly received Leucippe's letter, he had to pretend illness to postpone the fulfillment of her desires. Then Melitte sent for her so-called Thessalian slave Lacaena (really Leucippe) and begged her to concoct a philtre that would arouse Clitophon's feeling. She is very outspoken about the fact that Clitophon seems made of iron or wood ; that indeed she seemed to love a statue.[28] And she had the ability to express to Clitophon every feeling she had without inhibition and in most picturesque language. At her wedding breakfast in Alexandria she punned merrily about the postponement of their union. "I've heard of a cenotaph but never before of a cenogam."[29] The bellying sail on the ship she compared to a pregnant woman's body ; indeed she converted the whole ship into symbols of marriage.[30] She also compared herself to thirsty Tantalus standing by a river but not allowed to drink. She could match Clitophon's arguments and his quibbles did not deceive her : "You are playing the sophist, dearest !" she commented. When from the discovery of Leucippe's letter to Clitophon and her husband's safe return she knew that she had lost Clitophon, she visited him secretly in prison and poured out on him all her wrath and all her passion. Her denunciation of him as eunuch, hermaphrodite, senile nonentity shifted to adoration ;

[28] V. 22.
[29] V. 14.
[30] V. 16.

and passion finally concentrated into so ardent and well argued an appeal for one embrace that she was victorious. Clitophon admitted ironically that love had taught her rhetoric and that he was vanquished, so he gave the remedy to a sick soul and even on the prison floor enjoyed her ! [31]

Melitte was no less subtle and plausible in the speech in which she made her peace with her enraged husband Thersander : Clitophon was only one of many refugees whom she aided in memory of her husband lost at sea ; indeed she had helped Clitophon to find his wife.[32] When Thersander challenged her by the ordeal of the water of the Styx, Melitte at once accepted the test on a quibble because her husband had demanded from her an oath that she had not fulfilled the rites of Aphrodite with the stranger *during the time while he himself was abroad.* And it was just that unfortunate stipulation which makes her last appearance in the romance unforgettable. She is led out of the water of the Styx by the judge, proved by indisputable ordeal a chaste woman ! Achilles Tatius has won his readers by this time to rejoice in Melitte's vindication. For besides charm and cleverness he has given her humanity and generosity. She was always merciful to her slaves and was kindness itself to Lacaena-Leucippe.[33] After she had won her desire, she contrived the escape of Clitophon from prison dressed in her clothes, and financed by her. She did not even forget the jailer, but gave him money to go away for a time to avoid punishment.[34] Clitophon omitted in his final narrative of his adventures his succumbing to Melitte [35] but he had the grace to admit to himself her charms.

It is clear that in the ethics of the romance there is a

---

[31] V. 25–27.
[32] VI. 9–11.
[33] V. 17, 22.
[34] VI. 1–2.
[35] VIII. 5.

new point of view.   Achilles Tatius is definitely less idealistic than Chariton in his treatment of the erotic theme.
As Rattenbury has pointed out :

"Achilles Tatius seems to have felt that the fetish of
chastity in the average romance was absurd, and tries to
humanize romance by creating characters that are rea-
sonably, not unreasonably, moral. . . . Leucippe comes
through safe and sound, it is true, but it was by good luck
rather than by good intention."   Clitophon is chaste as far
as men can be and succumbs to Melitte only once.   "Achilles Tatius," continues Rattenbury, "did not exactly parody
his predecessors, but it is suggested that by attempting to
humanize romance he not only showed up the absurdities
of the usual stories, but was also responsible for the over-
throw of the literary form. . . . Achilles Tatius seems to
have been to Greek Romance what Euripides was to Greek
Tragedy.   He broke down the conventions, and drove the
essential and permanent elements to seek refuge elsewhere.
The erotic element did not die, but found an outlet in
'Love-Letters,' a contemporary literary form of which
Aristaenetus was an exponent in the fifth century, but
the idealized love story of a superhumanly modest hero
and heroine vanished, and Greek Romance hibernated
until it was revived some centuries later by the Byzantine
writers." [36]

Not inconsistent with Tatius' slightly ironic treatment
of amours is his emphasis on the virtue of pity and his
tendency to introduce long philosophical discussions of
conduct or the nature of love.   Clitophon's story moves
an Egyptian general to pity, tears and aid, for

"When a man hears of another's misfortune, he is inclined
towards pity, and pity is often the introduction to friendship ; the
heart is softened by grief for what it hears, and gradually feeling

[36] R. M. Rattenbury, *op. cit.*, pp. 256–57.

the same emotions at the mournful story converts its commiseration into friendship and the grief into pity." [37]

In the midst of Thersander's attempt to rape the weeping Leucippe, there is a long digression on tears and the pity they arouse.[38] Clinias appeals to the court not to put to death "a man who deserves pity rather than punishment." [39] Leucippe, disguised as a slave, begs Melitte as a woman to pity a woman and to pity one once free, now through Fortune's will a slave.[40]

Tatius has presented also in Callisthenes a picture of a noble young hero who was converted from the wildness of youth to self-control, respect, patriotism and service by chivalrous love.[41] And this portrait of Callisthenes becomes an embodiment of an ideal latent in the philosophical discussions of love which flavor the romance. "Love," says Clitophon, "inspired by beauty enters the heart through the eyes." [42] Later Clinias tells Clitophon that he is greatly fortunate in being able to see his lady, for when eyes of lovers meet, the emanations of their beauty wed in a spiritual union that transcends bodily embrace.[43] Clitophon, wooing Leucippe in a fair garden, discourses to her on the power of love over birds, creeping things, plants, even iron which responds to the magnet, over water (for Arethusa and Alpheus wed).[44] To cheer up Menelaus and Clinias on ship-board and divert them from their sorrows, Clitophon starts a philosophic discussion on love of women compared with love of men, untranslatable in its openness.[45] Menelaus takes up the cudgels for the love of men, probably much to Clinias' satisfaction for he had previously denounced to his dear Charicles the love of women who, if they love, kill and had arraigned for his

[37] III. 14.
[38] VI. 7.
[39] VII. 9.
[40] V. 17.
[41] VIII. 17–19.

[42] I. 4.
[43] I. 9. Compare V. 13.
[44] I. 16–18.
[45] II. 35–38.

indictment Eriphyle, Philomela, Sthenoboea, Chryseis, Briseis, Candaules' wife, Helen, Penelope, Phaedra, Clytemnestra ! [46]

The worship of the kiss is featured in an enchanting story of a magic charm breathed on the lover's lips [47] and a fantastic assertion that if a maiden's kiss is stolen, the maid is raped.[48] Moreover a code of love is presented, almost as detailed as Ovid's *Ars Amatoria,* in instructions given by Clinias to Clitophon,[49] by the slave Satyrus to Clitophon,[50] by Clitophon in discussion with Menelaus.[51] A delightful part of this Art of Love is telling the Lady love-stories, for all womankind is fond of myths.[52] Magic too plays its part in the technique of love, for incantation works a charm for a lover ; [53] philtres may bewitch the indifferent ; [54] and ordeals test chastity.[55]

Closely akin to the philosophical discussions of love, its power, its art, its magic is the worship of Aphrodite, the mother of Eros.   Yet there are few references to her cult. Her dominance is hinted : initiation into love makes Aphrodite the most powerful of gods.[56] Melitte wishes to have her nuptials on the sea, for Aphrodite is the sea's daughter and she wishes to propitiate her as the goddess of marriage by thus honoring the sea, her mother.[57] Clitophon at the end of his separation from Leucippe prays to Lady Aphrodite to forgive the long delay in their union, for it was due to no insult to her and he begs her blessing on their marriage.[58] The story of the ordeal by the water of the Styx [59] is a merry tale of rivalry between Artemis and Aphrodite for a young girl's worship in which Aphro-

46 I. 8.
47 II. 7–8.
48 IV. 8.
49 I. 10.
50 II. 4.
51 II. 37.
52 V. 5.

53 II. 7–8.
54 IV. 8–10, 15–17, V. 22, 26.
55 VIII. 5–7, 11–14.
56 II. 19.
57 V. 16.
58 VIII. 5.
59 VIII. 11–12.

dite made young Rhodopis break her oath of chastity but Artemis changed her into a spring in the very cave where she lost her virginity. Yet Achilles Tatius presents no such deep-seated reverence for the goddess of Love as that which permeates Chariton's romance.

Artemis of Ephesus is rather the deity who dominates Tatius' story. She appears in dreams to the heroine and to Leucippe's father.[60] In her name Leucippe rebukes Thersander for insulting a virgin in the city of the Virgin Goddess.[61] Sostratus arrives at Ephesus as the head of a sacred embassy in honor of Artemis and so finds his daughter.[62] Leucippe has taken refuge in the temple of Artemis and in that temple at last she and Clitophon are reunited.[63] Here the villain of the piece Thersander brutally attacks Clitophon.[64] Thersander's lawyer in court makes insulting slanders about the fact that Clitophon and Leucippe probably defiled the temple by an amour there.[65] But Artemis is proved to be no liar, and there is implicit recognition of her protection of Leucippe though Achilles Tatius does not end with thanksgiving to her. Her cult forms an objective background of religious tradition for the action. No deep religious feeling for her is manifested.

There is no more aspiration to god in the other cults which are mentioned incidentally : of Apollo, Hercules of Tyre, the god of the lower world, Pan. And the cruel goddess Fortune is berated only occasionally. Superstition recognizes omens in the world of nature : the eagle stealing the sacrifice, the hawk pursuing the swallow.[66] Oracles are respected.[67] And the ordeals of Pan's pipes and the Styx's water receive general credence. Festivals

[60] IV. 1 ; VII. 12.
[61] VI. 21.
[62] VII. 12.
[63] VII. 12.

[64] VIII. 1–3.
[65] VIII. 1–3, 5, 10.
[66] II. 12 ; V. 3.
[67] II. 14.

to the gods are celebrated.[68]   But religion seems rather a matter of scrupulous regard for ritual than communion with god or relief to the soul.

As we compare the romances of Chariton and Achilles Tatius we find that not only has the main interest shifted from love and worship to incidents and adventures.   An even greater change has come about in the style.   Homeric simplicity has given way to rhetorical elaboration. Tatius may well have been a ῥήτωρ as the scholiast Thomas Magister states, for his whole style is dyed in the rhetoric of the schools and the speeches delivered in the various lawsuits in the plot are masterpieces of rhetoric.

Among his acknowledged literary debts, however, he credits most to epic, for he quotes Homer once [69] and alludes to him five times [70] and he refers to Hesiod twice.[71] The messenger speeches in tragedy undoubtedly suggested the slave's dramatic narrative of the death of Charicles in a riding accident.[72]   Both the New and the Old Attic Comedy contributed much to his humor : the New in the comic literary contest of the slaves Conops and Satyrus who deride each other under cover of fables ; [73] and the Old in the Aristophanic priest of Artemis who "was no poor hand at speaking, and as good at quip and gibe as the plays of Aristophanes." [74]   But the training of the rhetorical schools outweighs all other influences.   About half of Books VII and VIII is devoted to the trial of Clitophon for adultery and self-confessed murder.   The court sits in Ephesus with a jury and a presiding judge, but their functions are vague.   The prosecution speaks first, Thersander and his ten lawyers, whose speeches fortunately are not reported.   Clitophon answers them by a false narra-

[68] II. 2 ; V. 2 ; VI. 3–4.
[69] II. 36.
[70] I. 8 ; II. 1, 15, 23, 34.
[71] I. 8 ; IV. 4–5.

[72] I. 12.
[73] II. 20–22.
[74] VIII. 9.

tive accusing himself of the murder of Leucippe and involving Melitte.   Clinias gets the floor and tells the true
story : that Clitophon desires only to die, that he deserves
pity rather than condemnation and must be regarded as
insane.

In the wild confusion that follows, Thersander's counsel shouts for a sentence of murder, Melitte offers her slaves
to be questioned on her innocence and demands that her
husband produce Sosthenes who is probably the murderer.
Thersander in a long speech answers Melitte's challenge
about Sosthenes with the result that the presiding officer
pronounces sentence of death on Clitophon but postpones
Melitte's case.   Clitophon is just on the point of being
tortured for evidence when the arrival of a sacred embassy
to Artemis postpones the case of Melitte and the execution
of Clitophon.

Only after the work of the embassy is finished is the case
resumed.   Then Thersander speaks first, demanding the
execution of the sentence.   He condemns the priest who
has released Clitophon and says he has usurped the function of giving refuge to criminals which belongs to Artemis.   He adds foul personal abuse.   He presents a second charge against Melitte for adultery and a third against
his slave girl Leucippe and her father.   The priest in his
reply deserves the epithet "Aristophanic" which he has
won, for he pays Thersander back in his own coin of abuse
only clothing it in the wit of Aristophanes with all his
double-meaning of words, his biting attack.   And his own
arguments point the irony of the situation : Thersander
clapped Clitophon in jail before he was allowed to defend
himself.   He charged him with murdering Leucippe but
the young lady is alive !

Sopater, counsel for Thersander, next hurls insulting
invective at the priest and whitewashes his noble client

who has been betrayed by a faithless wife. Thersander then presents a formal challenge to Melitte and Leucippe to prove their chastity and on their acceptance of it, the court adjourns. Next day all reassemble at the cave of Pan and the spring of the Styx. The ladies are proved innocent. Thersander flees and then is sentenced to banishment. Clitophon — and Melitte — are acquitted.

This summary of the procedure of the court in Ephesus shows what opportunity Achilles Tatius made for presenting the rhetorical speeches which he cherished. They are many. They are full of specious argument, personal attack, appeal to the emotions, attempted pathos which becomes bathos and genuine ἦθος. The speakers are true to type : the impassioned lover, the leal friend, the haughty, imperious, lustful noble, his sophistical lawyer, the Aristophanic priest. Such agonistic scenes must have entertained the reader of the time as much as they did the author. Actually this same favorite rhetorical style is also assigned to the characters in private life : Melitte in her impassioned speech to Clitophon in prison talks like a sophist, for Eros teaches even arguments ! [75]

Long mythological narratives are another feature of Tatius' style. The sight of a painting makes it necessary for him to relate the whole story of Procne and Philomela to Leucippe.[76] The stories of the origins of the two ordeals to prove chastity are told with equal detail. The discovery of wine is elaborately related in the Tyrian version on the occasion of the festival of Dionysus.[77] These are a few out of many illustrations.

Descriptive writing is employed as much as, perhaps more than, forensic or narrative. Indeed the purple patches almost overbalance plot, conversation and oratory.

[75] V. 27.
[76] V. 5.
[77] II. 2.

Works of art, setting for scenes, natural phenomena, the wonders of the world are introduced in highly colored digressions which are clearly the ekphraseis which the students of rhetoric were taught to compose and deliver.

Achilles Tatius apparently was enamored of wall-paintings. He describes with gusto five and alludes to another. The subjects of all are myths. Two are familiar types in the frescoes found at Pompeii : Perseus and Andromeda, Achilles in women's clothes among the daughters of King Lycomedes. One description of a painting opens the romance, a votive painting of Europa in the temple of Astarte at Sidon.[78] Sidon is the first word of the novel and this story is introduced as a tribute to the city where the first scene was laid, for the stemma on the coins of Sidon is Europa on the bull, pictured almost as Tatius presents her. The picture is described in vivid detail even to the flowers in the meadow and the shifting colors of the sea. Posture and garb of Europa are vividly sketched in words for he sees her "seated on the bull like a vessel under way, using the veil as a sail." The keynote of the picture and the point of its application for Tatius is the little flying Eros who leads the bull and laughs back at the transformed Zeus. "Look," said Clitophon, "how that imp dominates over land and sea." A young man standing by exclaims that he too has suffered much from love. These exclamations are the point of departure for the recounting of love adventures.

In Book III there is an equally long description of a painting by Evanthes in the temple of Zeus Casius.[79] The subjects are Andromeda and Prometheus and they seem to have been paired because both were chained to rocks, menaced by beasts and rescued by Argive heroes, Perseus and Hercules. Design, color, emotion are all described

[78] I. 1–2.   [79] III. 6–8.

vividly and charmingly, but there is no point in the introduction of the paintings. The description of them is
simply a purple patch of fine writing.

In Book V the description of a painting in a studio de-
picting the rape of Philomela had "a hidden significance." [80] The whole story was represented : "the rape
of Philomela, the violence employed by Tereus, and the
cutting out of her tongue . . . the tapestry, Tereus himself, and the fatal table." Ugly realism, terror, insane
laughter characterize the treatment. The hidden meaning is that the sudden sight of the picture is a bad omen
threatening disaster which makes Clitophon postpone his
journey to Pharos. The delay gives him a chance to tell
the whole story of Philomela to Leucippe, for all women
love myths.

Small works of art also are described lovingly and mi-
nutely : a rock-crystal goblet carved in a grape-vine,[81] a
jewelled necklace.[82] These enrich the setting as scattered
flowers enrich the backgrounds of Renaissance tapestries.
It is as though Achilles Tatius like Corinthian potters or
Renaissance artists had such an *horror vacui* that empty
spaces in design were intolerable and interstices had to be
crowded with beautiful small objects. This is due in part
to an observant eye that saw and recorded detail. The
specific and the graphic are his tools for clarity. The
story of the attempted amour of Clitophon and Leucippe
is vivified by a plan of the house as clear as the drawn plans
in many modern detective stories.[83] The garden in which
Clitophon's love-making is once set is described elaborately
with its porticoes, trees, vines, flowers, spring and birds.[84]
The storm at sea in its violence and coloring is as lurid as a
Turner, and its effects on the shipwrecked passengers are

[80] V. 3–5.
[81] II. 3.
[82] II. 11.
[83] II. 19.
[84] I. 15.

described with a true psychology of terror and panic.[85]

The long description of the storm is justified by the vital significance of the shipwreck for the plot, but what of the write-ups of the wonders of the world which are constantly introduced ? The beautiful description of Alexandria with its pharos is brief and pardonable as this was the birthplace of the author. But only the love of novelty of the times and bad taste seem to explain the perpetrations of wordy descriptions of the Nile, the phoenix, the hippopotamus, the elephant and the crocodile ![86] The romance at times tends to become a natural history. Wolff becomes so out of patience with "the damnable iteration" of irrelevancies in *Clitophon and Leucippe* that he can hardly calm himself to analyze them in suggestive groups : irrelevancies of plot, of characterization, of setting, of science and pseudo-science. The only justification for such irrelevancies Wolff finds in "a common basis with paradox. Both defeat expectation . . . In both its phases, — irrelevancy and paradox — this element of *the unexpected,* prominent in the form as in the matter of the Greek Romances, deserves attention. To turn aside to the irrelevant ; to strain suspense by retarding the expected outcome ; to introduce by the way — all unlooked for — as many bizarre, ironical, paradoxical situations and dazzling phrases as possible ; and finally to 'spring' an issue which is itself a surprising combination of opposites — all these would seem to be consistent results of adopting the unexpected as the principle of the genre." [87]

After all this is said in criticism of Achilles Tatius' exuberant style and unlimited digressions, we go back to his fundamentals : a clear plot, living human beings, vivid settings for them, and exciting adventures. Achilles Ta-

[85] III. 1–5.
[86] IV. 11–12 ; III. 24–25 ; IV. 2–3, 4, 19.
[87] S. L. Wolff, *op. cit.,* pp. 202–11.

tius knew his age and for its disillusions he wrote with ironic tolerance of human frailty and for its weariness he emphasized the excitement of adventure and the stimulus of the unexpected. To me his successes chalk up to a longer list than his failures and I end with Phillimore :

"What a strange thought — that an Alexandrian with the names of Achilles Tatius (what a pair !), atticizing *con furore* in the reign of Diocletian, should write a story which delighted the Byzantine Middle Ages and can still be read with interest and amusement !" [88]

[88] J. S. Phillimore, *op. cit.*, pp. 115–16.

VI

THE LESBIAN PASTORALS OF DAPHNIS AND CHLOE

BY LONGUS

THE VERY title of Longus' romance shows a new departure. These Lesbian Pastorals in four books form the only pastoral romance in Greek that is extant. Compared with the other romances that of Longus is unique in type, characters, setting and structure. Theocritus is the pervading influence. Most of the leading characters are not nobles but serfs. Even the young hero and heroine are brought up as shepherds until at the end they are recognized as children of the great. City life plays little part in the plot. The changing seasons make the set. Only a few adventures disturb the serenity of the hills and pasturelands : an onset of pirates, a local war and (of course !) the usual kidnappings. Country gods are worshipped. The music of Pan's pipes is the accompaniment of the story.

Of the author we know nothing. Longus "is not mentioned by any other writer before the Byzantine age, and himself mentions no historical name or event." [1] From internal evidence of his novel we see that he knew Mytilene well ; he was familiar with Greek and Roman literature and with works of art ; he had received a sophist's training

[1] F. A. Todd, *Some Ancient Novels*, London, 1940, p. 35.

in the rhetorical schools. He wrote probably in the second century A.D., before Achilles Tatius.

The early editions and translations show why Longus was so influential in Elizabethan England and indeed in the modern European literatures. The first edition of the Greek text was published by the Junta Press in Florence in 1598, but before that the romance had received its first printing in Amyot's French translation in 1559 and in the first English translation by Angell Daye in 1587. This "earliest English version" which was dedicated to Queen Elizabeth was more of an adaptation than a translation. Its title-page demands perusal :

"Daphnis and Chloe excellently describing the weight of affection, the simplicitie of love, the purport of honest meaning, the resolution of men, and disposition of Fate, finished in a Pastorall, and interlaced with the praises of a most peerlesse Princesse, wonderfull in Maiestie, and rare in perfection, celebrated within the same Pastorall, and therefore termed by the name of The Shepheards Holidaie. By Angell Daye. Altior fortuna virtus."

The title-page of the 1657 translation by "Geo. Thornley, Gent." was dubbed "Daphnis and Chloe a most sweet and pleasant pastoral romance for young ladies" and it too bore a Latin motto : "Humili casa nihil antiquius nihil nobilius. — Sen. Philos."

It is this delightful old translation which J. M. Edmonds "revised and augmented" in his version for *The Loeb Classical Library* and in his introduction there Edmonds says that this seems to have been George Thornley's only publication. He was a sizar in Christ's College and received his Bachelor in Arts from the University of Cambridge. It is this translation of Edmonds-Thornley which I shall use in my quotations.

Longus wrote a Prooimion to his romance which reveals the occasion and the purpose of his writing. While hunting in Lesbos he saw in a fair grove of the Nymphs a painted picture which told a tale of ancient love.

"There were figured in it young women, in the posture, some of teeming, others of swaddling, little children ; babes exposed, and ewes giving them suck ; shepherds taking up foundlings, young persons plighting their troth ; an incursion of thieves, an inroad of armed men."

And on studying the painting Longus says :

"I had a mighty instigation to write something as to answer that picture. And therefore, when I had carefully sought and found an interpreter of the image, I drew up these four books, an oblation to Love and to Pan and to the Nymphs, and a delightful possession even for all men. For this will cure him that is sick, and rouse him that is in dumps ; one that has loved, it will remember of it ; one that has not, it will instruct. For there was never any yet that wholly could escape love, and never shall there be any, never so long as beauty shall be, never so long as eyes can see. But help me that God to write the passions of others ; and while I write, keep me in my own right wits."

With this delightful prayer, our humorous nympholept Longus begins his story. We must now outline briefly his four books of Pastorals.

The characters are:

Daphnis, a young goatherd
Lamo, foster-father of Daphnis
Myrtale, foster-mother of Daphnis
Chloe, a young shepherdess
Dryas, foster-father of Chloe
Nape, foster-mother of Chloe
Dorco, an oxherd
Philetas, an aged shepherd and a famous piper
Lycaenium, a city chit married to a swain
Dionysophanes, lord of the manor
Clearista, his wife
Astylus, his son
Gnatho, a parasite of Astylus
Lampis, a herdsman
Tyrian pirates
Young nobles of Methymna

In Lesbos near Mytilene there was a great estate of a great noble. On it once strange things happened for a goatherd Lamo found a fine baby boy being nursed by a she-goat. Purple was his cloak and near him was a little golden sword with an ivory handle. Lamo and his wife Myrtale reared the child and named him Daphnis. Two years later another shepherd Dryas found in a cave sacred to the nymphs and carved with pictures of them a baby girl being nursed by a sheep. And beside her were little possessions, a girdle embroidered in gold, gilded shoes, golden anklets. Dryas and his wife reared the child and named her Chloe. These are our hero and heroine.

Now when Daphnis was fifteen and Chloe thirteen, one night both Lamo and Dryas had the same dream. The nymphs of the cave appeared and gave Daphnis and Chloe to a certain little winged boy with bow and arrow who touched them with an arrow and ordered that Daphnis tend a flock of goats and Chloe a flock of sheep. Their parents were disappointed that they too were to become herdsmen, for they had given the children a good education, but they offered sacrifice in the cave to the Boy and obeyed.

The year was at the spring. Birds were singing, lambs gamboling, flowers blooming. The children too sang and danced together and made garlands of flowers for the Nymphs. All their joy and work they shared. But into this paradise came danger. Trap-ditches had been set to catch a marauding wolf and into one, as he pursued a he-goat, fell Daphnis. He was drawn up all bloody and must needs wash in the cave of the Nymphs. Chloe as she washed his back thought she had never seen any-one so fair or touched anything so soft. Love began here though she knew it not.

Another danger menaced. Dorco an oxherd who had

helped draw Daphnis from the pit fell in love with Chloe
(he was a full-grown lad) and when he could not get her by
gifts, he and Daphnis held a contest of words for beauty
and Chloe was umpire. When their speeches were finished, Chloe at once gave to Daphnis her prize — a kiss —
and that kiss made Daphnis fall in love though he did not
know what love was.

Defeated Dorco next appealed to Dryas for Chloe as a
wife, but Dryas rejected him. Then he tried a base trick.
He dressed up in a wolf-skin and hid near the spring where
the beasts watered, hoping to meet Chloe alone there.
This he did, but the sheep-dogs caught him first and would
have killed him had not Chloe and Daphnis saved him.
They thought Dorco's disguise was only a game, for they
never dreamed of rape in their innocence.

So through spring and summer Daphnis and Chloe
tended their flocks and played the pipes together. But in
the autumn Tyrian pirates descended on the shore to
raven. They wounded Dorco and stole his cows and kidnapped Daphnis. Dorco dying gave his pipe to Chloe for
one kiss at last and bade her pipe his cows off the ship.
And the cows on hearing the call of the pipe jumped over-
board and swam ashore with Daphnis charioted between
two holding to their horns. The boat was upset and the
pirates who were all in armor drowned. Daphnis and
Chloe went to poor Dorco's funeral. They dedicated his
pipe to the Nymphs. They cheered their flocks who lay
mourning for Daphnis on the hills. And all went on as
before except that Daphnis' heart ached, — why he did
not know.

Now (in Book II) came the time of vintage. These
charming children helped pick the grapes, tread the wine-
press, fill the vats with the new wine. That work done,
back to their flocks went Daphnis and Chloe. There old

Philetas met them and sitting down told them a bright story of how Eros had appeared to him in his garden, a little winged boy flitting birdlike from tree to tree. And Philetas tried to teach the children who Eros was and what was his power, for Philetas had loved Amaryllis in his youth. But though Philetas as a wise *praeceptor amoris* instructed them thus : "There is no medicine for love, neither meat, nor drink, nor any charm, but only kissing and embracing and lying side by side," the children did not understand his teaching and played this game of love without fulfillment. And as they exchanged childish kisses, disaster again broke upon them.

Some young nobles of Methymna put in at the shore in a gallant boat to make holiday, fishing and hunting with their dogs. When a country fellow stole the rope that tied up their ship, they carelessly made another of green withes. Then their dogs while hunting frightened Daphnis' goats and drove them down to the shore and some finding no other fodder ate up the green cable. At that a strong wind off shore blew the boat out to sea to the great rage of the young Methymnaean owners. They beat up Daphnis in a fight with the peasants in which they too were wounded and prosecuted him in court, but Philetas was the presiding judge and acquitted the goatherd of any wrong. The incensed young nobles made their way home by land and persuaded Methymna to avenge their injuries by sending a fleet to the land of Mytilene in an unannounced war. The army plundered and devastated and right from the sacred cave of the Nymphs kidnapped Chloe. But such sacrilege was not to be unavenged by the gods and the Nymphs appearing in a vision to distraught Daphnis assured him that Pan would protect their votary. And indeed Pan sent awful omens to the Methymnaeans : the sound of the clashing of unseen weapons ; the sight of

ivy sprouting on the horns of Daphnis' stolen goats and of
a crown of pine placed on Chloe's head while all her
stolen sheep howled like wolves.   And the sea had its marvels : anchors stuck, oars broke, while a strange military
piping filled the air.   Finally Pan appeared to the admiral
and demanded the return of the maid stolen from the altar
of the Nymphs and the return of her herds and flocks.   So
the terrified commandant put about and restored Chloe
to the land.   What a story she had to tell Daphnis !   What
sacrifices and libations the rustics offered to Pan and the
Nymphs !   Philetas too arrived to help them.   Lamo told
them the story of the invention of Pan's pipes which a Sicilian goatherd had sung to him.   And on his own great
pipes Philetas played the different calls for the herds and
the song of Dionysus.   Daphnis and Chloe acted out
Lamo's story of Pan and Syrinx.   The next day back to
their flocks went the children and they talked now of their
love for each other and took mighty oaths of faithfulness
for life and death, Chloe swearing by the Nymphs, Daphnis
by Pan.   But since Chloe knew Pan for an amorous and
faithless god, she made Daphnis take a second oath by the
trusty goats that he would match her faithfulness with his.

Now (in the beginning of Book III) war enters the story,
for the Mytilenaeans were incensed at the actions of the
Methymnaean fleet and sent a land expedition under Hip-
pasus for reparations.   But this war was conducted in a
manner worthy of the golden age without ravaging of
country, with speedy offer of satisfaction, with cordial ad-
justment of terms.

Winter now arrived, more bitter than war to Daphnis
and Chloe.   Their flocks were shut in folds ; they were
secluded in their separate farm-houses.   But while Chloe
learned to spin and found no comfort, Daphnis built a
plan on hope.   Braving the snow he struggled to a bird

center near Chloe's home, as if he went fowling. Yet when he had reached his goal and snared many birds, he dared not approach the farm-house for lack of excuse. But Dryas chasing a dog who had stolen some meat rushed out-doors, met Daphnis and brought him home.

Chloe in her glad surprise gave him a kiss ; and all made him welcome. Daphnis was persuaded to spend the night to celebrate with them on the next day their sacrifice to Dionysus. In the morning the lovers found a few moments alone in which to renew their troth, and after that Daphnis came often thither through the winter months.

Then spring came ; the flocks were once more sent to pasture. Daphnis and Chloe crowned their gods with flowers and honored them with piping. They watched the goats mate and wished to mate too, but knew not how. A city woman, Lycaenium, married to a swain, heard their childish talk and being half enamored of Daphnis undertook to complete Philetas' instruction in the art of love and having had experience she taught him all. But he put off using his new knowledge. Instead he told Chloe the story of Echo.

Many suitors now wooed Chloe, and Daphnis in despair told Myrtale, his foster-mother, how he too longed to wed the girl, but his suit seemed hopeless until to desperate Daphnis once more the Nymphs appeared and told him where to find a purse of money that had been cast ashore from the Methymnaean ship. With the three thousand drachmae in it he won over Dryas and Nape, who in turn persuaded his father and mother to accept the match. But Lamo wished the marriage postponed until the lord of the manor arrived in the autumn to give his consent. Now that they were affianced Daphnis and Chloe waited happily. Daphnis plucked for Chloe a golden apple that hung unplucked on top of a tree, the best of all, a symbol of the victory of love. And in return he received a kiss more precious even than an apple of gold.

Now (in Book IV) with the autumn and the vintage the lord Dionysophanes was coming with his wife Clearista to inspect his estate. Lamo's pride was the beautiful garden he had made, so it was a major disaster when a rejected suitor of Chloe, churlish Lampis, devastated it for spite. Lamo besought Astylus, son of Dionysophanes, to appease his father's wrath and this he did.

Astylus had a rascally parasite Gnatho with him who tried to corrupt Daphnis, but in vain ; so hoping for the future he persuaded Astylus to induce his father to take Daphnis back to the city as his son's servant. At this menace Lamo decided he must reveal Daphnis' origin so he brought out the tokens he had found with the child. They proved that he was the son of Dionysophanes and Clearista, exposed by them when they were young and thoughtless and had too many children. So the young shepherd was transformed into a prince and almost forgot Chloe. Indeed while he was celebrating she was carried off by Lampis, the herdsman. Gnatho, seeing Daphnis' despair, to reinstate himself, dashed off and rescued Chloe just in time. Now her foster-parents produced her tokens and her nobility too was assured. All went to Mytilene to find Chloe's parents. The Nymphs and Eros appeared to Dionysophanes in a dream and Eros bade him to make a great marriage feast and there to display Chloe's tokens. This he did and by them Chloe too found noble parents. But Daphnis and Chloe chose to have a country wedding and went back to the fields to their rustic friends.

Indeed most of their lives they lived there in the simple way of shepherds, worshipping the Nymphs, Pan and Eros, possessing great herds of sheep and goats, and for food liking best of all apples and milk. There they had a son and daughter whom a goat and a sheep nursed ; Philopoemen and Agelaea were their names. They made the cave into a fair shrine, set up statues there, raised an altar to Eros the shepherd and gave to Pan the soldier a temple to dwell in instead of a pine. All this was long afterwards. Now they had a rustic wedding. The shepherds played their rude pipes for their Hymenaeus. Daphnis and Chloe slept no more than the birds that night and Chloe then first learned that all their love-making in the wood was only the play of children.

This brief epitome of the plot shows its simplicity and its coloring. The scene is pastoral and a unity of place is observed which distinguishes the romance. All the action takes place in the country near Mytilene. Only for the episode of the search for Chloe's parents do the characters move to the city and their sojourn there is short.[2] The main events of the plot are the double exposures, the adoption and the recognitions of Daphnis and Chloe and their common life as shepherds. The plot contains the usual features of a romance but virtually all are adapted to the pastoral tone and there is a change in their relative importance. The chief interests are the same as in the other romances : love, adventure, religion. But love is in its springtime : it buds and blossoms in the lives of two innocent children as the eternal miracle of nature.[3] The adventures are for the most part simple country disasters : Daphnis falling into a trap-ditch set for a wolf ; a fair garden wantonly destroyed by a jealous rival. There are to be sure two kidnappings, but the rescues are speedy and magical. Daphnis is saved from the Tyrian

[2] G. Dalmeyda, *Longus, Pastorales (Daphnis et Chloé)*, Paris, 1934, pp. xxi–xxii.

[3] Dalmeyda, *op. cit.*, p. xxiv, "un des plus grands charmes de son roman est le cadre de nature, et l'intime union du décor et des personnages : dans ce sol plaisant et fertile, les deux héros semblent avoir leurs racines comme de jeunes plantes."

pirates by the music of a shepherd's pipe. Chloe's return
by the Methymnaeans is compelled by Pan himself. Even
war is conducted with noble generosity and given a peaceful solution as if in a golden age.

Adventure indeed plays a far smaller part in the romance than does religion. Worship is heartfelt and a part
of life. The gods honored are deities naturally worshipped
in the country : the Nymphs, Pan, Dionysus and Eros.
They are ever-present.

Longus in his Preface says that he made these four books
as a votive to Eros, the Nymphs and Pan. The baby girl
was exposed, nursed by a sheep and found by a shepherd
in the cave of the Nymphs.[4] At critical moments in the
lives of the hero and heroine the Nymphs appear in visions
to guide or save. In Book I Lamo and Dryas, the foster-
fathers, had the same dream the same night : they saw the
Nymphs consign Daphnis and Chloe to the care of a young
winged boy who touched both with the same arrow and
bade each tend the flocks.[5] After Chloe was kidnapped by
the Methymnaeans from the very cave of the Nymphs, the
three goddesses appeared to Daphnis in a vision by night
and told him not to fear, for Pan of the pine-tree would
rescue the maid.[6] Again when for his poverty Daphnis
saw that Chloe was to be betrothed to some richer suitor,
the Nymphs appeared and told him where to find a purse
of silver.[7] Finally Chloe's noble parentage was discovered by the direction of the Nymphs and Eros who appeared to Dionysophanes in his sleep and bade him make
a wedding feast in Mytilene and at it pass Chloe's tokens
about to all the guests.[8]

Such solicitous and tender care had been won by Daphnis and Chloe through devotion. Out on the hills in the

[4] I. 4–5.
[5] I. 7.
[6] II. 23.

[7] III. 27.
[8] IV. 34.

morning first of all they saluted their gods. They gathered flowers to crown their statues. They made them gifts of grapes and apples or of pipe. They sacrificed to them kids and lambs, and to the Nymphs and Pan they offered constantly their prayers and vows. In the cave of the Nymphs Chloe swore to share life and death with Daphnis. Under the pine Daphnis swore by Pan that he would not live a single day without Chloe.[9]

Eros is a less familiar god to the children, but through Philetas' instruction about the merry flying boy they come to be his votaries.[10] Dionysophanes gives all praise for the care of the children to the united protection of Pan, the Nymphs and Eros.[11] The betrothal takes place before the statues of the Nymphs.[12] And all their lives Daphnis and Chloe worshipped the Nymphs, Pan and Eros for their very present help in time of trouble.[13] This was no formal ritual : it was a vital faith offered with clean hands and a pure heart.

The worship of Dionysus also entered into the life of the whole countryside. The song of the God of Wine is played by Philetas and danced by Dryas. The festival of Dionysus is celebrated by the sacrifice of a ram, a feast, libations poured by ivy-crowned worshippers. In the garden of the great estate of Dionysophanes there are an altar and a shrine to the god, and the temple had paintings about the life of Dionysus : Semele his mother, the sleeping Ariadne, the binding of Lycurgus, the rending of Pentheus, the conquered Indians, the transformed Tyrians, Pan piping to those treading the wine-press and to those dancing.[14] On the first day after he arrived at his estate Dionysophanes made sacrifice to this god for whom he was named along with the other rural deities, Demeter,

9 II. 39.
10 II. 4–7.
11 IV. 36.

12 IV. 37.
13 IV. 39.
14 IV. 3.

Pan, the Nymphs.[15]   And Daphnis for his happiness dedicated his bag and cloak to Dionysus, to Pan his whistle and
his pipe, to the Nymphs his crook and milk-pails.[16]   The
god of the vintage must always have his share of honor in
the country.

So because the gods are omnipresent in country life, religion is as much a part of the set of the romance as is locality. For the monotony which might result from the
single background of the great estate near Mytilene in
Lesbos is varied not only by descriptions of fair garden,
pastures, trees, hills, seashore, but by the mystic vicinity of
the cave of the Nymphs, the pine-tree of Pan, the grape-
vine of Dionysus and over all the unseen flying Eros shooting his darts.

With such a setting, naturally the order of events follows the seasons.   In spring the story begins when the lad
of fifteen and the girl of thirteen are sent out to tend the
flocks in meadows and on hills.   Summer brings the adventures of the trap-ditch and the Tyrian pirates.   Autumn has its vintage and the menace of the Methymnaean
roisterers.   Winter houses and separates the lovers until
Daphnis makes bold to go fowling.   Spring returning,
Daphnis finds a purse and wins his shepherdess' hand.
Summer passes in tending the flocks and making love.
Then as autumn again brings the vintage the lord of the
manor comes to his estate.   There follows the recognition
of Daphnis as his son and soon Chloe is found to be as
noble.   The weather is still fair, so after a royal feast in
the city, the wedding is celebrated in the country for their
hearts were rural.

Indeed the characters are for the most part country
wights : the worthy foster-parents, Chloe's suitors, Philetas the wise old herdsman.   They are all serfs and Daphnis

<hr>

[15] IV. 13.   [16] IV. 26.

and Chloe were given pastoral names by their foster-parents to make them seem truly theirs. They are noble slaves full of hospitality and kindness. When corruption menaces and brings temptation, it comes from the city. Lycaenium is a young bride from the city. Gnatho is a city parasite. Astylus, the son of Dionysophanes, although he is a great-hearted youth who pities Lamo for the destruction of his garden and welcomes his newly found brother Daphnis with open arms, shows the effects of city life by making his boon companion the worthless parasite Gnatho whose only thoughts were of eating, drinking and lechery. Dionysophanes is nobler than his son : though gray-haired, he is still tall, handsome, able to wrestle with young men, and though wealthy he is good. Indeed some virtue must be attributed in this fairy-story even to the villains. Dorco who tried to rape Chloe makes a beautiful end by giving her his pipe and teaching her how to call the cattle and Daphnis back from the raiders' ship. Gnatho redeems himself by rescuing Chloe from her second kidnapping. And even Lampis, the rough herdsman, was deemed worthy of forgiveness and invited to the wedding. Daphnis and Chloe are brave, beautiful and virginal. Chloe keeps her chastity to the end. Daphnis sins but once, to learn what love is that he may teach his maid.

Dalmeyda has pointed out another striking feature of the plot beside the unity of place and the strictly pastoral coloring. This is its two-part division of which the first might be entitled "the search for love" and the second "the marriage of Chloe." The first part ends with the lesson of Lycaenium, the second with the country wedding.[17]

Within this two-part division and the unified pastoral scene, the usual devices are employed for the pattern of

[17] Dalmeyda, *op. cit.*, pp. xxvii–xxxi.

the romance, conversation, soliloquies, oaths, court-room
speeches, happy ending, but all are simplified to a country
standard. Typical of what I mean is the breath-taking
conversation that the lovers secure alone after their winter
separation, λόγων ὁμιλία τερπνή.[18]

"Chloe, I came for thy sake." "I know it, Daphnis."
" 'Tis long of thee that I destroy the poor birds." "What
wilt thou with me ?" "Remember me." "I remember
thee, by the Nymphs by whom heretofore I have sworn in
yonder cave, whither we will go as soon as ever the snow
melts." "But it lies very deep, Chloe, and I fear I shall
melt before the snow." "Courage, man ; the Sun burns
hot." "I would it burnt like that fire which now burns
my very heart." "You do but gibe and cozen me !" "I
do not, by the goats by which thou didst once bid me to
swear to thee."

The soliloquies too are as artless and simple as this talk.
At some emotional crisis the youngsters bemoan to themselves their lot. Chloe, falling in love with Daphnis when
she sees him bathe in the cave of the Nymphs, laments the
pain in her heart that is worse than a bee-sting.[19] After
Daphnis has been recognized as the son of the great Dionysophanes, Chloe weeps at being forgotten, is sure Daphnis
is breaking his oath of faithfulness and bids him farewell
since she will surely die.[20] Daphnis makes moan more
often. When the kiss of Chloe has set him on fire, he com-
plains that his heart leaps up ; his soul is weakened ; he
will waste away with his strange malady.[21] Over the
sleeping Chloe he murmurs a soft rhapsody.[22] Shut in
alone by winter he takes counsel with himself on what excuse to end their separation.[23] And when he hears that

[18] III. 10.
[19] I. 14.
[20] IV. 27.
[21] I. 18.
[22] I. 25.
[23] III. 6.

Lampis has carried Chloe off, he seeks solitude in the garden and rails at his bitter loss.[24]   Even the court-room speeches in the prosecution of Daphnis by the Methymnaeans for the loss of their ship are reduced to short and simple arguments since a herdsman sat as judge.[25]   The trial of course ends happily for Daphnis as must inevitably the whole story.   Of all the love romances this springtime love in the country is the most joyous.

As we read this pastoral romance, the unknown author becomes to us a real personality.   His delight in the country is spontaneous and real.   He is a cultured person with genuine appreciation of art, music and literature.   Their influence enriches his story.   Longus in his preface tells how a painting which he chanced to see in the grove of the Nymphs gave the inspiration for the writing of his novel, for the painting pictured a history of love and he longed to write something that would correspond to the picture. Paintings again he mentions in his description of a shrine of Dionysus, paintings telling all the myths of the god.[26] The images of the Nymphs in the cave are described carefully by him : cut out of the rock they were, feet unshod, arms bare to the shoulders, hair falling on their necks, their garments belted, a smile in their eyes.[27]   A statue of Pan stood under his sacred pine until at the end Daphnis and Chloe built him a shrine.[28]   Over and over these representations are referred to as symbols of very present gods.

The music that fills the romance is the sound of the shepherds' pipes and the voice of song.   Daphnis makes a pipe of reeds and teaches Chloe how to play on it.[29]   So well did she learn that on Dorco's pipe she could call the

[24] IV. 28.
[25] II. 15–17.
[26] IV. 3.

[27] I. 4 ; II. 23.
[28] II. 23–24 ; IV. 39.
[29] I. 10 and 24.

cattle back from the raiders' ship.[30] When spring brought
them out-doors, both Daphnis and Chloe challenged the
nightingales with their piping and the birds answered.[31]
Philetas the old herdsman outdid all in playing on the
great organ-pipe of his father. He played special strains
for cows and oxen, for goats, for sheep. He played too
the melody of Dionysus and to it Dryas footed the dance of
the vintage. Daphnis too played on Philetas' pipe a love-
song and danced with Chloe the story of the origin of the
pipe, Pan's wooing of the maid Syrinx.[32]

Daphnis displayed his art for his own father and mother,
before he was recognized as their son, to do them pleasure.
He blew the call of the goats ; he blew their soft lullaby ;
he blew their grazing tune ; he blew the alarm for a wolf ;
he blew the recall. And the goats responded to all his
different strains.[33] After the wedding the shepherds
piped the bride and groom to bed and sang outside their
door a rude, harsh song, no Hymenaeus, but such as they
were wont to sing when with their picks they broke the
earth.[34] For country people sang at all their tasks : the
boatman on the river,[35] the herdsman in the pastureland.

More pervasive than all other influences in the romance
is the literary. Theocritus colors the whole story. There
are a few reminiscences of Bion [36] and Moschus,[37] but it
was the Sicilian goatherd par excellence who instructed
Longus as he did Lamo in his story.[38] Calderini shows
the various traces of the inspiration which Longus received
from the Alexandrian idyl. There is a continuous alter-
nation of descriptions of nature with descriptions of emo-

[30] I. 30.
[31] III. 12.
[32] II. 35-37.
[33] IV. 15.
[34] IV. 40.
[35] III. 21.

[36] Cp. II. 4 with Bion IV.
[37] Cp. I. 18 with Moschus I. 27.
[38] II. 33. See on the bucolic tradition, Dalmeyda, *op. cit.*, p. xxiii with
n. 4.

tion all composed with a certain serenity and restraint.
The pain is not too violent ; the descriptions of nature are
not too detailed or pedantic. There are many special
similar motives : the descriptions of paintings and statues ; the fear and the protection of Pan and the Nymphs ;
the vengeance of Eros on those who scorn him ; the young
lovers who frequent the gymnasia and the palestra ; love
which is born on the day of a festival ; the woe of love ; the
violent, brutal love of a scorned shepherd ; the patron who
lives at a distance.[39]   The pastoral name Daphnis is taken
from the ideal shepherd of Theocritus and Vergil.   Pastoral setting and pastoral narrative have the flavor of Theocritus.   Episodes are identical : Chloe plaits a tiny cage
for a grasshopper as did the young lad carved on the bowl
of ivy-wood.[40]   Daphnis and Chloe as they sit kissing each
other on the hill see a fisherman's boat passing on the sea
and listen to his song.[41]   So in Theocritus lovers on the
land embracing look out at the far distant sea.[42]   But
above all, Longus saw as Theocritus did that in the lives of
herdsmen lay true romance, and while Theocritus sang his
short lays, closely affiliated with the mimes in their use of
the comic, Longus lifted the love of goatherd and shepherd to the realm of pure fiction by idealization and tenderness.   His originality was in making young love grow
with the seasons to maturity.   The name of his heroine,
Chloe, a young green shoot, is symbolic of this growing
life.[43]   His awareness of his unique contribution to romance perhaps appears in his title : *The Lesbian Pastorals of Daphnis and Chloe.*

Sappho too was known and cherished by Longus.
There is a possible reminiscence in the description of

[39] Calderini, *op. cit.,* pp. 169–70.   [41] III. 21.
[40] Theoc. I. 45–56.   [42] Theoc. VIII. 53–56.
[43] Horace is the only other ancient writer who uses the name Chloe, C. I. 23 ;
III. 7, 9, 26.

Daphnis turning paler than grass in its season.[44] There is
a sure reminiscence of Sappho's hyacinth on the mountains crushed by the feet of the passing shepherds in Lamo's
pity for his flowers trodden down by a marauder.[45] And
to Sappho Longus owes the climax of Daphnis' wooing at
the end of Book III when he pulls "the sweet apple which
reddens upon the topmost bough," saved by Fortune for a
shepherd in love, and putting it in Chloe's bosom makes
it a symbol of her beauty and his prize.[46]

Drama too had a definite influence on Longus, indeed
the word δρᾶμα or δραματικόν is applied to these romances by
Photius.[47] The two recognition scenes in which Daphnis
and Chloe find parents through the tokens placed with
them when they were exposed as babies are copied from
tragedy. New Comedy furnished at least three characters
to the romance, Gnatho the parasite, Sophrone the nurse
who exposed the baby Daphnis [48] and the city wench, Lycaenium. Elegiac poetry furnished Philetas, the father
perhaps of erotic elegiacs. Echo repeating the name of
Amaryllis suggests Vergil.[49] And Ovid perhaps contributed three names : Astylus, Dryas and Nape.[50] The influence of the rhetorical schools is slighter than in the other
romances, but appears in the court-room scene with its
speeches and in the use of parallelism and contrast. Parallelism, as Calderini says,[51] includes all the plot of the romance and proceeds from the number and selection of
the characters to the variety of the secondary episodes and
to the description of the smallest details. Daphnis and
Chloe are both exposed, both rescued by shepherds. Both
are kidnapped. An attack on Chloe is made by Dorco,

44 I. 17, with Courier's excellent
emendation of the ms. χλόης (for
χλόας) to πόας, Sappho 2.
45 IV. 8, Sappho 94.
46 III. 33-34, Sappho 93.
47 J. M. Edmonds, *Daphnis and*

Chloe in *The Loeb Classical Library*,
p. xi, n. 1.
48 Dalmeyda, *op. cit.*, pp. xxxiv–v.
49 II. 7, Vergil *Ec.* I. 5.
50 J. M. Edmonds, *op. cit.*, p. ix.
51 Calderini, *op. cit.*, pp. 145-47.

on Daphnis by Gnatho.   Chloe touches Daphnis when he
is bathing and falls in love.   Daphnis kisses Chloe and his
heart rises to his lips.   Astylus, the city son of Dionysophanes, is sophisticated, Daphnis is virginal.   The oath
of Daphnis is matched by the oath of Chloe.   On and on
proceeds this balancing.   And the parallelism appears not
only in plot, but in details of phrase and sentence structure : balanced rhythmical phrases set off by rhymes or
alliterations ; bipartite or tripartite periods, elaborate in
their rhetorical structure.   Sometimes indeed Longus'
Pastorals seem written in modern verse, indeed they are
written in poetic prose.[52]

Out of all these interests in art, music and literature
and beyond them Longus has created a style peculiarly his
own and suited to his pastoral romance.   His sentence
structure is simple and paratactic.   His comparisons are
drawn from the life of shepherds.   Chloe is as restive as
a heifer.[53]   Dorco claims he is as white as milk but Daphnis
says Dorco is as red as a fox.[54]   Daphnis and Chloe run
about like dogs freed from their leashes.[55]   Chloe plunders
from Daphnis' mouth a bit of cake as though she were a
young bird being fed.[56]

Description and narration are as vivid as these little
similes.   We are made to see Daphnis at his bath : his
hair black and thick, his body sun-burned dark as though
colored by the shadow of his hair ; [57] the coming of spring
with flowers covering the valleys and the mountains, bees
humming, birds warbling, lambs gamboling ; the vintage
scene with the peasants all busy in the vineyard with the
wine-presses, the hogsheads, the baskets, and the grapes ; [58]
the winter landscape with the deep snow, the rushing tor-

[52] Dalmeyda, *op. cit.,* pp. xxxviii–
xlii.
[53] I. 13.
[54] I. 16.

[55] II. 2.
[56] III. 20.
[57] I. 13.
[58] II. 1–2.

rents, the ice, the laden trees ; [59] the country wedding with the feast on beds of green boughs before the cave of the Nymphs, the songs of the reapers and the vintners, the dancing to the pipes, the goats sharing the feast, the bridal procession with its piping and singing.[60]

Longus' art of narration is employed as skillfully as are his descriptions.   This art appears not only in the pattern of the whole romance, but in the skillful use of stories within the story to diversify and enliven the longer narrative.   After the feast of Dionysus, the old men, their tongues loosed with wine, fell into reminiscence and told tales to each other :

"how bravely in their youth they had administered the pasturing of their flocks and herds, how in their time they had escaped very many invasions and inroads of pirates and thieves. Here one bragged that he had killed a wolf, here another that he had bin second to Pan alone in the skill and art of piping." [61]

That last was Philetas, the wise old shepherd who told Daphnis and Chloe the story of the gay little Eros whom he had found playing in his garden flying like a nightingale from bough to bough of the myrtles, a lovely story with a point for Philetas' *ars amatoria*.[62]   The other inset stories are mostly short myths.   So Daphnis tells Chloe how the mourning dove was once a maid, very proud of her singing and by her song alone she kept the cows she tended near her in the wood.   But a shepherd lad rivalled her music and piped off eight of her finest cows to his own herd.   And the girl in despair prayed to become a bird. The gods consented and left her that sweet voice so still she calls the cattle home.[63]

At the feast of Dionysus Lamo tells a myth which a Sicilian goatherd had sung to him, a tiny tale of how the

[59] III. 3.   [62] II. 3–6.
[60] IV. 37–39.   [63] I. 27.
[61] II. 32.

girl Syrinx fleeing Pan's embraces was changed into a reed and then made by Pan into his pipe, with reeds of unequal lengths to symbolize their ill-matched love.[64] All these stories are very short and simple, bits of folk-lore such as peasants might relate at their feasts or in the open.

Much of the whole narrative is colored by a humor that is as playful and tender as the spirit of Philetas' merry child Eros. In the vintage scene both Daphnis and Chloe are beset with childish jealousy at the attentions that each other receives.[65] The author's humor plays around them from the time when they first herded their flocks together to the day of their rural wedding. And the plot is set with humor, which as Wolff observes, turns on "the incongruity between the children's innocence and the piquancy of their experiments." [66]

It is not strange that Longus' Pastorals with all their charm of plot, setting and style were the forerunners of much later literature. Todd has a paragraph which is a sign-post to the line of his successors.[67]

"Longus invented the pastoral romance, and his influence is found throughout the pastorals of the modern European literatures : already, perhaps, at the end of the fifteenth century, in the *Arcadia* of the 'Neapolitan Virgil' Jacopo Sannazaro ; in the *Aminta* of Tasso, in the *Astrée* of D'Urfé, in the *Gentle Shepherd* of Ramsay, in the *Paul et Virginie* of Saint-Pierre, and in other writings almost countless."

S. L. Wolff's elaborate study of *The Greek Romances in Elizabethan Prose Fiction* analyzes in detail Longus' influence on Robert Greene in *Manaphon* and *Pandost* and Shakespeare's use of Longus in the pastoral setting, the hunt scene, the exposure motif in *The Winter's Tale*. There is rich material still left in the study of the Greek Romances for the young scholar working in Comparative

64 II. 34.
65 II. 2.
66 S. L. Wolff, *op. cit.*, p. 162.
67 F. A. Todd, *op. cit.*, p. 64.

Literature. By them, by all students of literature *Daphnis and Chloe* deserves to be read and reread. For Longus, just as Theocritus did in the Idyl, immortalized in the realm of fiction the loves and woes of shepherds.

It is strange that a pastoral romance of such honest and simple charm should have played a dramatic part in a melodrama of the early nineteenth century. Yet it did, for it almost caused an international literary warfare ; it almost had a French officer shot for desertion ; and it created serious political complications for him with the Bonaparte family.

Paul Louis Courier (1773–1825) led a bizarre life as a vine-grower, an officer in the artillery, a liberal pamphleteer, a member of the Legion of Honor, a prisoner in Sainte-Pélagie, a traveller, a poet, a Hellenist. Throughout his checkered career, he anticipated Byron in his romantic passion for the antiquities, the ruins, the beauty of Greece. In 1811 he wrote from Rome : "The fact is that I wish before I die to see the lantern of Demosthenes and drink the water of the Ilissus."

It was this passion combined with his disgust at the butcheries of Wagram that made him forget that he was a soldier so that in 1809, though he was the head of a squadron of artillery, he slipped out of military life and in Italy devoted all his time to those literary studies to which before he had given his leisure.

Reared in the country (at Méré in Touraine), he had early become fascinated with the pastoral romance *Daphnis and Chloe* and now he was determined to work on a Thirteenth Century Greek manuscript of it which was in the Laurentian Library. After some difficulty he obtained permission from the librarian, Francesco Furia, and his work started happily. It was to meet with the greatest success and the greatest disaster. Courier, amateur that he was, discovered that the Laurentian manuscript contained the text of the great lacuna in Book I (cc. 12–17). These chapters were lacking in all other manuscripts. Furia who had worked for years on the manuscript, which was in parts nearly illegible, had never noticed these hitherto unknown chapters. They contain the episode of Daphnis tumbling into the trap-ditch, Chloe's falling in love with him thereafter, and the contest of Daphnis and Dorco for Chloe's kiss.

Close on Courier's great discovery followed a most unfortunate episode, for after carefully copying the new chapters Courier obliterated them by a black ink stain. It was natural that the jealous Furia should believe that Courier had intentionally upset his ink-pot over them. Courier himself in a letter to Renouard declared that inadvertently he had used as a marker some paper which was soaked in ink on the under side, and that made the blot.

The rage of Furia might itself have hindered the publication of Courier's discovery and now a political complication arose as a new obstacle. Since the fame of his work was spreading, Elisa Bonaparte, the sister of Napoleon, wished to have Courier's publication dedicated to her and the prefect of Florence, the Baron Fauchet, announced her gracious wish at a formal dinner-party! Courier, who by now hated all Bonapartes, cut his Gordian knot by rushing out at Florence a Greek edition in fifty-two copies before the French edition which he was publishing at Paris appeared in 1810. The deed was done and neither Furia nor la Bonaparte could undo it.

The fame and scandal of Courier's work of course came to the ears of the Ministry of War and orders were sent to General Sorbier, commandant of the artillery in Italy, to demand from Courier explanations of his absence from his squadron. Fortunately the general accepted Courier's affirmation that he had never thought of deserting so that the Hellenist escaped being shot then, but fate pursued him.

On April 11, 1825, the body of Paul Louis Courier was found in a wood near his country home at Véretz. He had been assassinated. It was long believed that this was a political crime, "a kind of epilogue of secret vengeance in party politics" as Edmond Pilon puts it.[68] It might also have been the revenge of a philologist. Actually the shooting was the result of an embroglio with certain servants on his estate. Courier in 1814 had married Mlle Herminie Clavier, who managed his estate in his absence. She seems to have betrayed him both in business matters and affairs of the heart so that Courier separated from her and made new plans for the management of the estate. Five years after the murder the Department of Justice found that the assassins were certain servitors of Courier who had been dismissed because of their connivance with Madame Courier in her iniquities. Courier, whose dearest dream had been the pastoral life of Daphnis and Chloe, escaped the dangers of war and of prison only to be shot in the country he loved for petty personal spite.

Paul Louis Courier would, I am sure, have been happy to have part of his fame rest on his precious new chapters of the Pastorals, and to know that his beautiful translation of their four books lives on in one new edition after another.

---

[68] Paul-Louis Courier, *Les Pastorales de Longus ou Daphnis et Chloé*, traduction de Messire Jacques Amyot revue, corrigée, complétée et de nouveau refaite in grande partie, Paris, 1925, *Preface*, p. xxii. See also *Bibliographie*.

VII

LUCIAN AND HIS SATIRIC ROMANCES: THE TRUE HISTORY AND LUCIUS OR ASS

"Lucian of Samosata [was] surnamed 'The blasphemer,' because in his dialogues he alleges that the things told of the gods are absurd. . . He was at first an advocate in Antioch, but, having ill success in that, he turned to the composition of discourses, and his writings are innumerable. He is said to have been killed by dogs, he having been rabid against the truth. For in his 'Life of Peregrinus' he attacks Christianity and, wicked man, blasphemes against Christ himself. Wherefore for his madness he suffered meet punishment in this life, and hereafter with Satan he will be inheritor of the everlasting fire." [1]

THIS is the meagre biography by Suidas of the great satirist who through nearly all of the second century held up the mirror of his frankness to reflect images of the Greek and Roman world. Suidas' misrepresentation of Lucian's allusions to the Christians and his fanciful picture of the sophist's end vilify much of this traditional vita. From Lucian's own writings more facts may be assembled.

Syrian by birth, he wrote in Greek and became a master of an Attic prose style. As a boy he was apprenticed to a sculptor uncle, but quickly left work with his hands for work with his tongue, studied rhetoric and oratory, practiced as an advocate at Antioch, became a professional sophist and travelled in Asia Minor, Macedonia, Greece, Italy, Gaul ; about A.D. 165 settled at Athens where he lived

[1] Suidas, as quoted in the *Enc. Brit.* XIV. Vol. 14, p. 460.

twenty years, then near the end of his life took an official post in Egypt under the Emperor and wrote an Apology for so doing. Suidas' description of his writings as "innumerable" seems justified by the eighty-two prose works extant to say nothing of two mock tragedies and fifty-three epigrams, now considered spurious.

Though the great bulk of Lucian's writings consists of Platonic and satiric dialogues, he enters into the scope of this book as a writer of the satiric or parody romance. For two of his writings, the *True History* and *Lucius or Ass,* establish for us this new type of Greek romance. His *True History* is a parody of all travellers' tales from Odysseus' to such as those of Antonius Diogenes in *The Wonderful Things beyond Thule.* Probably this work of Lucian had more literary influence than any of his other writings. His other romance, of which we have only an epitome, *Lucius or Ass,* is, I believe, a parody of the romance motivated mainly by religion. Its greatest value in its present syncopated form is that it outlines a contemporary Greek counterpart of the famous Latin novel, Apuleius' *Metamorphoses,* and furnishes us with a touchstone for testing the pure gold of Apuleius' originality.

Before, however, we can discuss Lucian's art of narration in his two romances, we must reconstruct from his own writings his literary autobiography and his conceptions of his literary art. Only then when we have met the critic self-criticized will we be competent to appreciate his brilliant imaginative flights in his novels.

A dangerous temptation at once assails any one who starts to write on any subject connected with Lucian. That is to attempt to cover the whole field of his life and works because of the brilliancy of the many-sided facets of his genius. A forcible deterrent is the fact that a masterly appreciation of *La vie et les œuvres de Lucien* has already been written by Maurice Croiset in his *Essai* [2] which in richness and style alike is worthy of its great theme. All subsequent studies of Lucian are inevitably founded on M. Croiset's appreciation.

Gildersleeve, following Croiset, pointed out that Lucian's life must be reconstructed from his own writings. And this within the scope of a brief essay Gildersleeve did brilliantly for English readers fifty years ago.[3] From another angle I am attempting to do this same thing now in order to make us acquainted before we read his stories with Lucian the story-teller.[4]

Lucian's early life is pictured in a brief speech called *The Dream*. This was probably delivered in his native Syria on his return after his European lecture-tour which made him famous as a Sophist. In a whimsical mixture of fact and fancy he describes his choice of a career. As a young lad when he had just finished school, Lucian was apprenticed to his mother's brother, a sculptor, to learn to be "a good stone-cutter, mason and sculptor." On his first day he struck a slab of marble so hard that he shattered it. Whereat his uncle gave him such a violent beating that he ran home to his mother for comfort. That night he had a vision. Two women were struggling to get possession of him. They were vastly different in appearance and in the appeals they made to him, for they were Sculpture and Education. Sculpture, unkempt, speaking haltingly and like a barbarian, told Lucian that if he came to her, he would live well, have strong shoulders, would never go abroad, but would gain such fame as surrounded Phid-

[2] Maurice Croiset, *Essai sur la vie et les œuvres de Lucien,* Paris, 1882.

[3] Basil L. Gildersleeve, *Essays and Studies,* Baltimore, 1890.

[4] For a concise tabular classification of Lucian's works, based on Croiset's arrangement, see H. W. Fowler and

F. G. Fowler, *The Works of Lucian of Samosata,* 4 vols. Oxford, 1905, I, xiv–xviii. To be specially noted are the influences in definite periods of the rhetoricians, of philosophy, of New Comedy, of Menippus, of Old Comedy.

ias, Polyclitus, Myron, Praxiteles. Education in her turn assured him that even if he became a famous sculptor, he would be only a mechanic, living by his hands ; she herself has much more to offer him.

"If you follow my advice, first of all I shall show you many works of men of old, tell you their wondrous deeds and words, and make you conversant with almost all knowledge, and I shall ornament your soul, which concerns you most, with many noble adornments — temperance, justice, piety, kindliness, reasonableness, understanding, steadfastness, love of all that is beautiful, ardour towards all that is sublime ; for these are the truly flawless jewels of the soul. Nothing that came to pass of old will escape you, and nothing that must now come to pass ; nay, you will even foresee the future with me. In a word, I shall speedily teach you everything that there is, whether it pertains to the gods or to man." [5]

Moreover, he will dress with distinction, will speak with eloquence. Finally he may became as famous as Demosthenes or Aeschines. He must recall that Socrates left sculpture for philosophy.

Lucian on hearing these two appeals gave himself to Education, who then took him in a car with winged horses and from the air showed him the cities and peoples of the world. After this vision she clothed him suitably and returned him to his home. Lucian says he has told this dream "in order that those who are young may take the better direction and cleave to education, above all if poverty is making any one of them faint-hearted." [6]

Now although this choice of Lucian is based on the choice of Hercules [7] and although facts are clothed in fantasy, the picture of Lucian's early apprenticeship may well be true, for the boy's delight in modelling little figures of wax seems to forecast Lucian's life-long interest in sculpture and other art forms.

[5] Translated by A. M. Harmon, in *Lucian*, in *The Loeb Classical Library*, III, 223, 225.

[6] Harmon, *op. cit.*, III, 231, 233.
[7] Xenophon, *Memorabilia*, II, 1, 21.

The next crisis in Lucian's literary life is depicted in *The Double Indictment,* a dialogue composed when the author was forty. In it Lucian appears in court to answer two charges : one of the rhetoricians, for giving up speech-making and essay-writing ; the other of the philosophers, for using their sacred Platonic dialogue for satire. Lucian's trial takes place on the Areopagus with Justice presiding, but the dialogue opens in heaven with a long complaint by Zeus about the hard life of the gods especially his own, no time for anything. Hermes who is listening tells him frankly that there are many complaints among mortals on earth because of the slowness of the law courts. Zeus then sends Hermes down to proclaim a session and orders Justice to preside at it.

At this court, after various cases have been wittily disposed of, the Syrian is called to face two indictments : Oratory versus the Syrian for neglect, Dialogue versus the Syrian for maltreatment. Oratory first relates how she found the plaintiff as a lad wandering in Ionia, speaking with a foreign accent, dressed as a Syrian. She educated him and at his eager request married him although all his dowry was wonderful speeches. Next she had him made a citizen and then went travelling with him to Greece, Ionia, Italy and Gaul. As he became famous, he grew indifferent to her, for he was enamored of a bearded man, Dialogue, said to be the son of Philosophy. Now he no longer makes speeches, but has a strange way of using short questions. She sues him for desertion. The Syrian replies that all her facts are true, but there are others ; she lost her modesty, made up like a courtesan, flirted indiscriminately with many lovers. So he separated from her and went to live with a respectable gentleman, Dialogue. The Syrian won the case.

Next Dialogue pleaded. His dignity, his cosmic

thoughts, his tragic mask have all been stolen from him. He has been forced to associate with Jest, Satire, Cynicism, Eupolis and Aristophanes, "terrible men for mocking at all that is holy and scoffing at all that is right," finally too even with Menippus. He has been transformed into a monster not homogeneous but Centaur-like. The Syrian in reply showed the benefits which he had bestowed on Dialogue : he taught him to walk like a man, to clean up, to smile, to be yoked with Comedy. Dialogue resents that the Syrian will not indulge in endless arguments on subtle themes. The Syrian declares that he has not taken off Dialogue's Greek cloak and put him into barbarian garb : Dialogue is still dressed in his native Greek costume. The Syrian was unanimously acquitted much to the delight of the audience. This mock-trial picturesquely portrays Lucian's change from writing the philosophical dialogues in the style of Plato to the satiric dialogue, influenced successively by New Attic Comedy, Menippus and Old Attic Comedy.[8] Lucian here is writing an Apology for the new style of satire-dialogue which he created.

With similar wit but in various modes Lucian in other pieces satirizes now Rhetoric, now Philosophy. An illuminating series of such dialogues is *The Professor of Oratory, Nigrinus, Philosophies for Sale, The Fisherman.*

In *The Professor of Oratory* ironic advice is given to a young man on how to become an orator and a sophist. The quest is noble and the way to success is not difficult. The Lady Rhetoric sits fair and desirable on the top of a high mountain attended by Wealth, Fame and Power. Thither two roads lead. One is a narrow, steep and thorny path, the other an easy slope amid flowers and fountains. Two guides will present themselves to you. One, vigorous and manly, will point out to you the hard way in the

---

8 See M. Croiset, *op. cit.,* Chap. II.

footprints of Demosthenes and Plato and will tell how severe the training must be for their followers. He will wish, the simpleton, to make you model yourself on the past.

The other guide is a pretty gentleman, daintily groomed and perfumed, with an alluring smile and a honey voice. He will tell you that you can become such an orator as he is if you carry as equipment ignorance, boldness, shamelessness ; if you dress in bright, diaphanous robes and always carry a book ! Your course of study will be the memorizing of a few stock words, a few learned references for ornaments of your discourse. He will teach you a high singsong chant and the art of always beginning with stories from the Iliad.

Your fame will be secured by a well-trained chorus of applauders in your audiences and by slanders of all your rivals. In private life you must live fast with dice, wine and women, so you come to be talked of as a deuce of a fellow, and amours will increase your income. Thus you will be fitted to be the bridegroom of Rhetoric by driving furiously the winged chariot of which Plato wrote. Your adviser is already getting out of your way, for he was defeated when once you chose the primrose path. This picture of *The Perfect Rhetorician* has been thought by some critics to be a personal satire of the contemporary lexicographer Pollux. However that may be, it is certainly a satire of any pseudo-professor of rhetoric who bases oratory on cheap externalities and superficial training.

At another time Lucian was to satirize pseudo-philosophers as he had rhetoricians, but once, perhaps in the beginning of revolt against rhetoric, he chose to picture a noble type in the dialogue on Nigrinus, a philosopher unknown except through Lucian. His great tribute to Nigrinus may be set as a companion piece to the mocking

praise of *The Perfect Rhetorician.* The dialogue is pref-
aced by an introductory letter in which Lucian tells Nigrinus that he is not carrying owls to Athens in offering
him this book as if to display his use of words, but he is
sending it in thanks for Nigrinus' words.   In the dialogue
itself one man relates to another how by talking with Nigrinus he was made free instead of a slave, poor instead
of rich.   For Nigrinus praised philosophy and the freedom
it gives and ridiculed what men in general exalt : wealth,
fame, power, honor.   Nigrinus praised Athens because
there Poverty and Philosophy are foster-brothers ; there
life is free, noble, harmonious.   Rome is the city for those
who love wealth and luxury, wine and women.   The Romans have given themselves over to the pleasures of the
senses and have every means of gratifying them.   So Nigrinus in Rome leads a life of retirement, conversing with
Philosophy and with Plato, reflecting on the ridiculous
rich, the parasites, the pseudo-philosophers, the will-
hunters, the gourmands, the frequenters of the circus
and the baths.   No wonder men come to him for healing.

The tribute to Platonism here, the tribute to Epicurus
in *Alexander the False Prophet,*[9] might tempt readers to
affiliate Lucian with one or the other of these philosophical
schools.   But as if to forestall being labelled, in the spirit
of Horace's famous line

nullius addictus iurare in verba magistri,[10]

Lucian turns his satire on all the leading creeds of the
time in his *Philosophies for Sale.*

Zeus orders an auction of philosophies.   Hermes acts
as crier and auctioneer.   The buyer questions each person who is put up for sale on his knowledge, on his creed,
on his use.   A Pythagorean is put up first by Hermes who

[9] C. 47.   [10] Horace, *Ep.* I. 1, 14.

asks : "Who wishes to know about the harmony of the world and re-birth ?" The Pythagorean attempts to expound to the buyer the catharsis of the spirit, the need of music and of geometry, the flux of the cosmos, the divinity in numbers, the transmigration of souls. An Italian bought him for a brotherhood in Magna Graecia for ten minas.

A Cynic is next displayed, dirty, morose, ready to bark at everyone. He declares that Hercules is his model and that like Hercules he is a militant reformer, working to clear the world of filth. He declares that he will teach his purchaser to discard luxury, to endure hardship, to drink only water, to throw his money into the sea, to reject all family ties, to live in a tomb or a jar. So he will feel no pain even when flogged and will be happier than the Great King. He will be bold, abusive, savage, shameless. For such a life no education is necessary. The Cynic is sold for two obols.

The third called is the Cyrenaic, who appears clad in purple and crowned with a wreath. Hermes announces that his philosophy is the sweetest, indeed thrice blessed. As the Cyrenaic is too drunk to answer questions, Hermes describes his virtues : he is pleasant to live with, congenial to drink with, a companion for amours, and an excellent chef ! There was no bid for him !

Next two are put up together, the one who laughs and the one who cries. The first explains his laughter on the ground that all men and all their affairs are ridiculous ; all things are folly, a mere drift of atoms. The weeper pities men because their lives are foreordained and in them nothing is stable ; men themselves are mere pawns in the game of eternity and the gods are only immortal men. No one bids for the pair.

An Academic next advertises his wares as a teacher of the art of love, but claims that this love is of the soul, not of the body. He affirms that he lives in a city fashioned by himself, where wives are held in common, fair boys are prizes for valor, and realities are ideas, visible only to the wise. He was bought for two talents.

A pupil of the laugher and the drunkard is now offered for sale, namely Epicurus. The mere description of him as more irreverent than his teachers, charming, fond of good eating, sells him for two minas.

The sad philosopher of the Porch is now announced by Hermes who proclaims that he is selling virtue itself and that the Stoic is "the only wise man, the only handsome man, the only just man, brave man, king, orator, rich man, lawgiver, and everything else that there is." [11] His talk about himself is full of hair-splitting dialectics and subtle explanations of why man must devote himself "to the chief natural goods . . . wealth, health, and the like" [11] and go through much toil for much learning. In spite of all this he is bought for twenty minas.

The Peripatetic is also sold for twenty minas because he knows everything but the Sceptic brings in only one mina because he knows nothing ! The auction ends with the announcement by Hermes of another sale the next day of plain men, workmen, tradesmen.

Inevitably this ironic treatment of the great philosophies of Greece produced a storm of criticism. This was answered by Lucian in an apology of sorts under the title *The Resurrected or The Fisherman.* In it the satirist under the pseudonym of Frankness faces his accusers. For up from the dead, led by a militant Socrates, come to Athens Empedocles, Plato, Aristotle and other phantoms to exe-

[11] Harmon, *op. cit.,* II, 487, 495.

cute worthy dooms on the worst of maligners. Frankness by rhetoric and argument averts stoning or crucifixion and secures a fair trial, presided over by Philosophy, who is attended by Truth, Investigation and Virtue. After Diogenes makes the speech for the prosecution, Frankness replies in defense of himself — and Lucian ! He wins a unanimous verdict for acquittal by his claim that he auctioned off, not the great philosophers who now prosecute him, but base impostors who imitate them. Syllogism now acts as herald and calls from Athens to court all the philosophers to defend themselves. Frankness by promising largess secures a crowd of them, Platonists, Stoics, Peripatetics, Epicureans, Academics. When Philosophy announces that they are to be tried as impostors by herself, Virtue and Truth, they all disappear in wild rout. To get them back, Frankness now becomes a fisherman and, with bait of gold, hooks and hauls back the craven cheats. The head of each school disowns his imitators and the discarded are thrown down over the cliffs. Finally Philosophy dismisses the court with an injunction to Frankness to keep investigating philosophers in order to crown the true and brand the false.

The genial tone of *Philosophies for Sale* has entirely vanished in the essay on *The End of Peregrinus*. The influence of New Comedy and of Menippus with their ironic raillery is superseded by Aristophanic denunciation. Bitter mockery, cruel derision are loosed upon one creed, the Cynic. Lucian directs his vituperation against the Cynic philosopher Peregrinus, whose career had been meteoric. In his early life he was converted to Christianity, and even went to prison for his faith. Later, beliefs of India so possessed him that he immolated himself at Olympia just after the Olympic games of A.D. 165. Such self-sacrifice by cremation had been consummated at Susa

by Calanus before Alexander the Great and by Zarmarus
after initiation into the mysteries at Athens in the presence
of Augustus.

Lucian saw only one possible interpretation of Peregrinus' self-sacrifice, desire for notoriety, but there have
been many critics of this motivation as Harmon points
out : [12]

"Lucian believes himself to be exposing a sham, whose zeal was
not at all for truth but only for applause and renown.   Many notable modern critics, including Zeller, Bernays, Croiset, and Wila-
mowitz, dissent from his interpretation, discerning in the man an
earnest seeker after truth ; for to them thirst for glory is not an adequate explanation of his final act."

The piece is written as a letter to Cronius who is marked
as a Platonist by the formula of greeting εὖ πράττειν. Lucian begins with the fact of Peregrinus' self-imposed death
and at once ascribes to him the motive of love of notoriety.
This, he says, is proved by the fact that Peregrinus selected
for the time of his suicide the Olympic festival, which
draws great crowds. Lucian knows that Cronius will
have a good laugh at the foolishness of the old man so he
will write his friend just what he himself saw as he stood
near the pyre.

His method is clever. First Theagenes a Cynic proclaimed in the streets of Elis the glory of virtue and the
glory of her follower Proteus (Peregrinus) and announced
that Proteus was about to leave this life by fire in the manner of Hercules, Aesculapius, Dionysus and Empedocles.
Theagenes' justification of the deed went unheard because
of the noise of the crowd, but another orator (clearly Lucian) stepped forth and made a speech reviewing Peregrinus' career. Beginning with Democritean laughter he
narrated the life of Proteus accusing him of adultery as a

[12] Harmon, *op. cit.*, V, 1.

youth in Armenia, of corrupting a boy in Asia, of stran-
gling his own father, of becoming a Christian in Palestine,
of resigning all his property in Parium on the Hellespont,
of practicing the ascetic life in Egypt, of seeking notoriety
in Greece by denouncing Herodes Atticus for his aqueduct
at Olympia and later recanting. Finally, says Lucian, this
Proteus has announced his intention of cremating himself.
The motive is love of fame though he claims that he wishes
thus to teach men to despise death and endure torture.
He plainly hopes that myths and a cult will arise around
his memory. Indeed Theagenes has quoted a prophecy
to that effect, but Lucian can match that oracle with another which orders all the Cynic's disciples to imitate him
even to the last leap into the flames.

After these speeches, Lucian was on hand when the pyre
was kindled at Harpina near Olympia shortly after midnight. As an eye-witness he saw the pyre in a pit six feet
deep, Peregrinus in the dress of a Cynic bearing a torch,
men lighting the fire, how then Peregrinus stripped to his
old shirt and after crying : "Spirits of my mother and my
father, receive me with goodwill," leaped into the flames
to be seen no more. Even when the other Cynics stood
about the pyre in silent grief, Lucian felt no sympathy,
but taunted them brutally, and actually got into a broil
with them before he departed to meditate on how strange
the love of fame is. Lucian had to tell the story of Peregrinus' death over and over until to amuse himself, he
invented a vulture that he saw flying from the flames to
heaven, crying : "I have left the earth, I am going to
Olympus." And this invention of his became part of the
growing myth about the hero.

"So ended (wrote Lucian) that poor wretch Proteus, a man who
(to put it briefly) never fixed his gaze on the verities, but always did
and said everything with a view to glory and the praise of the mul-

titude, even to the extent of leaping into fire, when he was sure not to enjoy the praise because he could not hear it." [13]

Lucian concludes with anecdotes about Peregrinus sea-sick, in a fever, having eye-trouble and trying to cure fever and correct vision as though Aeacus in the lower world would care about either ailment. He was simply furnishing Democritus with more cause for laughter. This heartless ridicule of the Cynic's action takes no account of the psychology of fanaticism or the hysteria of martyrdom. Croiset points out that Lucian's insensitivity to all mysticism must be viewed with the knowledge that the satirist believed Peregrinus was a sham and that he was unveiling an impostor. Lucian's consistent worship of veracity and frankness then explain his derisive attitude towards the apotheosis of a pretender.[14]

The savagery used in exposing a false philosopher was turned by Lucian upon a religious fraud, Alexander of Abonoteichus. The piece is a letter to a friend, Celsus, written after A.D. 180, ten years after Alexander's death. Lucian's account gives almost all we know of this Alexander although his existence and influence are attested by gems, coins and inscriptions. The letter, however, as Croiset points out, contains more satire than history, for it does not attempt to distinguish scrupulously between the false and the true ; rather it presents in lively anecdotes and personal reminiscences a satiric portrait of an historical prophet.[15] Cumont has commented on the unique features of Abonoteichus' version of the worship of Aesculapius : the giving a serpent a human head and calling it the god incarnate ; the issuing of oracles and advice instead of using incubation or dealing particularly with healing.[16]

---

[13] Harmon, *op. cit.*, V, 47–49.
[14] M. Croiset, *op. cit.*, pp. 140–43, 188–92.
[15] M. Croiset, *op. cit.*, p. 82.

[16] F. Cumont in the *Mémoires couronnées de l'académie de Belgique*, Vol. XL (1887), summarized by Harmon, *op. cit.*, IV, 173.

Lucian exposes all Alexander's shams and corruptions. He describes his handsome appearance and education, his cleverness in purchasing a tame serpent and in selecting the site of Abonoteichus for his oracle. He describes the installation of the serpent, the invention of the human head for it, the exhibition of it, the methods of giving oracles, the prices, the publicity, the "autophones," cunningly contrived to issue from the serpent's mouth, the spread of his fame even to Italy. Lucian pictures too the perils that menaced any critics of the oracle, the burning of the sayings of Epicurus, the personal danger to himself. Lucian was advised by the governor of Bithynia and Pontus not to prosecute Alexander for his attempted murder so after the prophet's death he wrote this account to honor Epicurus and to present the truth to thinking minds. Personal revenge then as well as horror at religious fraud motivated this biography. Lucian, who derided Epicureans in *Philosophies for Sale,* chooses now to revere their founder !

One of Lucian's greatest works bears the title *Parasites for Pay.* It was written and undoubtedly read to the public in the last part of his life before he went to Egypt. It is not only very distinguished as a satire,[17] but in it as Gildersleeve points out [18] "his sensitiveness for Greek honor, for the honor of the people as well as for the honor of the literary class, manifests itself in a way to do infinite credit to Lucian's heart." Harmon calls it "a Hogarthian sketch of the life led by educated Greeks who attached themselves to the households of great Roman lords — and ladies." [19]

The satire is in the form of a letter addressed to a friend Timocles who is thinking of taking such a post. The case,

---

[17] M. Croiset, *op. cit.,* p. 131.
[18] Gildersleeve, *op. cit.,* p. 327.

[19] Harmon, *op. cit.,* III, 411.

says Lucian, is the same for philosophers, grammarians, rhetoricians, and musicians. The motives which apparently led men to accept such positions are poverty and pleasure, but their recompense is small and they have no share in the luxury that dazzled them. They overwork ; their expenses in clothing and tips eat up their stipends. Moreover their humiliations are incessant. The first dinner given in their honor brings the strain of observing proper etiquette. Next morning the conference about salary disappoints all hopes by the pittance offered. But a man sells himself and never afterwards can feel free or noble : he is a monkey with a chain around his neck. For he was not engaged to discourse on Homer, Demosthenes, Plato, but because it looks well to have a distinguished Greek philosopher with a long beard and a flowing robe in his master's suite. The day's routine of service is exhausting and humiliating, and the philosopher's rivals for his lord's favor are a gigolo, a dancing master, an Alexandrian dwarf who recites erotic verses. The night's sleep is shattered by meditations on lost freedom and present servitude.

Such is life in the city, but a trip to the country is worse. Thermopolis had to hold his lady's puppy for her in the jolting carriage and the miserable little dog kept licking his beard for relics of yesterday's dinner and finally laid a litter of puppies in the philosopher's cloak. Other services of the parasite include listening to the rich man's literary compositions and delivering a lecture on philosophy to the lady while her hair is being dressed or at the dinner-table. And in the midst of a discourse on virtue a maid brings her a letter from a paramour which she answers at once with a yes.

In time, envy and slander or the disabilities of old age cause the parasite's downfall and he is discarded on the rubbish heap. Such a career can best be depicted in a symbolic painting of a hill on whose summit golden Wealth resides. Hope, Deceit, Slavery help the traveller start on the ascent. But Toil then escorts him on. And finally Old Age, Insolence and Despair lead him until he is ejected by a hidden back door, naked, deformed, ruined. Repentance meeting him cannot save him. Timocles is urged before making his decision about the post offered him to meditate on this picture and on Plato's famous words : "God is not at fault ; the fault is his who maketh the choice." [20] This essay alone would justify Croiset's great tribute to Lucian's independence of thought : "among his contemporaries Lucian stands alone as an intelligence of a remarkable force and independence which nothing could tame." [21]

It was natural that, when later Lucian accepted a post in civil service in Egypt, he should anticipate reminders of his essay on *Parasites for Pay* on the part of his friends and foes. His *Apology* [22] answers their imaginary criticisms of his inconsistencies. It is written in the form of a letter to a friend. Lucian assures this Sabinus that he knows Sabinus enjoyed his recent essay on Parasites, but now must be full of amazement at his friend's accepting a salaried post in Egypt. He imagines receiving an epistle from Sabinus to this effect : [23]

"The difference between your precept and practice is infinitely more ridiculous ; you draw a realistic word-picture of that servile life ; you pour contempt on the man who runs into the trap of a rich man's house, where a thousand degradations, half of them self-inflicted, await him ; and then in extreme old age, when you are on the border between life and death, you take this miserable servitude upon you and make a sort of circus exhibition of your chains.

[20] Harmon, *op. cit.*, III, 481.
[21] M. Croiset, *op. cit.*, p. 176.
[22] Teubner text, I (1896), 319–27;

H. W. Fowler and F. G. Fowler, *The Works of Lucian*, II, 27–34.
[23] H. W. Fowler and F. G. Fowler, *op. cit.*, II, 29.

The conspicuousness of your position will only make the more ridiculous that contrast between your book and your life."

Lucian in reply suggests various lines of self-defense :
the compulsion of Chance, Fate or Necessity ; admiration
of his patron's character ; the drive of poverty, brought on
by old age and ill health.   But he rejects all these pleas.
His real defense is the difference between being a parasite
and slave in the house of a rich master and entering civil
service to work for the state.   Lucian explains the dignity
and the responsibility of the post he has accepted in the
service of the Emperor.

"What better use can you make of yourself than if you join forces
with your friends in the cause of progress, come out into the open,
and let men see that you are loyal and zealous and careful of your
trust, not what Homer calls a vain cumberer of the earth ?" [24]

Even this brief review of the writings which make up
Lucian's literary autobiography shows the conflicting
forces which strove for dominance over his life.   Sculpture and the Education of a Sophist first contended for
his favor and his choice of the orator's training never destroyed his life-long interest in art.   Oratory which secured his service soon disillusioned him because of her
cheap followers.   Plato and his philosophical dialogues
for a while controlled his mind and style, but, satire proving stronger in him than reflective thinking, he created a
new form of dialogue allied to Comedy and Menippus for
his medium of comment on the world.   This form and the
epistle he used for satirizing sophistry and oratory, philosophy and religion, always pointing out the counterfeit
and the sham and distinguishing them from the tested gold
of verities.   This same sort of touch-stone he applied in
his *Apology* to his own life to vindicate his maintenance
of personal freedom.   The traveller, the sophist, the sati-

24 H. W. Fowler and F. G. Fowler, *op. cit.*, II, 33.

rist, now become civil servant of the Emperor, admits no chain about his neck.

As regards his literary art he has revealed that his main ideals are frankness, truth and freedom. In his works he establishes warm human contacts with his hearer or reader. His Greek style achieves a pure Attic simplicity of expression and by it, as Croiset says,[25] he clothes abstract ideas in words which give them body and form. The main qualities of his style, spirit and imagination, unite in the effective descriptions and narrations which fill his works. His wealth of ideas found expression in realistic details noted with keen observation and assembled in realistic series to give vitality to his prose.

One work by Lucian is a specific treatise on writing and peculiarly significant for his literary autobiography. That is the essay on *How History Should Be Written*. It was composed as a letter to a friend Philo in the time of Marcus Aurelius and Lucius Verus. The occasion was the sudden spawning of a whole shoal of would-be historians after the Roman victories in the war with the Parthians (A.D. 165). Outraged by these scribblers, Lucian sets forth his thoughts on the True Historian.

Since the barbarian war began, says Lucian, everyone is writing history. It is just as when an epidemic of madness at Abdera made all the people chant tragedies. It recalls too Diogenes, who, when Corinth was in danger of a siege from Philip and the citizens were hurrying defense measures, kept rolling his jar up and down hill that he might seem as busy as the rest of the world. Lucian's advice will include the faults of historians which are to be avoided, the virtues to be cultivated.

History must not be written as panegyric. History must not be written as poetry. Among the faults of con-

[25] M. Croiset, *op. cit.*, p. 303.

temporary historians are lack of taste, over-abundance of details, purple patches, inaccuracies about facts.

"There are some . . . who leave alone, or deal very cursorily with, all that is great and memorable ; amateurs and not artists, they have no selective faculty, and loiter over copious laboured descriptions of the various trifles ; it is as if a visitor to Olympia, instead of examining, commending or describing to his stay-at-home friends the general greatness and beauty of the Zeus, were to be struck with the exact symmetry and polish of its footstool, or the proportions of its shoe, and give all his attention to these minor points." [26]

Indispensable qualities of the ideal historian are politi cal insight and ability in writing. His "one task is to tell the thing as it happened." [27] He will be "fearless, incorruptible, independent, a believer in frankness and veracity ; one that will call a spade a spade, make no concession to likes and dislikes, nor spare any men for pity or respect or propriety ; an impartial judge, kind to all, but too kind to none ; a literary cosmopolite with neither suzerain nor king, never heeding what this or that man may think, but setting down the thing that befell." [27] Thucydides fulfills this ideal.

In diction and style, the marks of the true historian are frankness and truth, lucidity and simplicity. The preface should be in proportion to the subject. "The body of the history . . . is nothing from beginning to end but a long narrative ; it must therefore be graced with the narrative virtues — smooth, level, and consistent progress, neither soaring nor crawling, and the charm of lucidity." "Brevity is always desirable." "Restraint in descriptions of mountains, walls, rivers, and the like, is very important." If a speech is introduced, "the first requirement is that it should suit the character both of the speaker and of the occasion." "It may occasionally happen that some ex-

[26] H. W. Fowler and F. G. Fowler, *op. cit.*, II, 123, C. 27.

[27] H. W. Fowler and F. G. Fowler, *op. cit.*, II, 128–29, CC. 39, 41.

traordinary story has to be introduced ; it should be simply narrated, without guarantee of its truth, thrown down for any-one to make what he can of it." The historian should write not for the present, but for eternity. He should hope to have said of himself : "This was a man indeed, free and free-spoken ; flattery and servility were not in him ; he was truth all through." [28]

Gildersleeve was probably right in calling the *True History* "a comic sequel to a brilliant essay entitled 'How to write History.'" [29] The traditional manuscript order which places the *True History* after *How History Should Be Written* seems so aptly prompted by Lucianic irony. For this romance in two books is not history at all and has nothing of Lucian's primary requirement for history, that it should be true ! It is a work of pure imagination, one of the earliest accounts of fictitious voyages and as such is part of the great tradition from the Odyssey to *Gulliver's Travels*.[30] Lucian's preface explains both the nature of the piece and his reasons for writing it.[31]

The *True History* like many good stories is told in the first person by Lucian himself. The author, moreover, preludes and interrupts the narrative to get in direct touch with his reader. In his introduction, he states that his purpose in writing is to furnish to students some reading that will give relaxation, but at the same time "a little food for thought." The story is bound to charm, Lucian thinks, because of the novelty of the subject, the humor of the plan, the plausible lying involved and the comical parodies of such authors as Ctesias, Iambulus, and Homer

[28] H. W. Fowler and F. G. Fowler, *op. cit.*, II, 133–35, CC. 54–61.

[29] Gildersleeve, *op. cit.*, p. 316.

[30] See Philip Babcock Gove, *The Imaginary Voyage in Prose Fiction*, New York, 1941.

[31] A secondary Preface to Book II may be found in *Babble Beforehand : Dionysus*. In it Lucian speaks of a literary novelty he is producing under the influence of Dionysus and Silenus, an old man's lengthy babbling.

in his Odyssey.   Lucian confesses to being a liar with the best of them, but affirms that his lying is unique in being honest because he admits it.

"Be it understood, then, that I am writing about things which I have neither seen nor had to do with nor learned from others — which, in fact, do not exist at all and, in the nature of things, cannot exist.   Therefore my readers should on no account believe in them." [32]

In spite of this confession, Lucian here and there in his story tries to create an atmosphere of veracity by protestations of it.   As he never saw the Corn Sparrow forces or the Crane Knights, he does not venture to relate the marvellous and incredible stories told about them.[33]   When he describes the magic mirror over a well in the Moon which furnished him television of his family and country he says that disbelievers by going there will find he tells the truth.[34]   In the Island of the Wicked, Lucian finds all liars, both those who had told lies on earth or written them, among the latter Ctesias and Herodotus.   "On seeing them," he says, "I had good hopes for the future, for I have never told a lie that I know of." [35]   The last sentence of the romance is : "What happened in the other world I shall tell you in the succeeding books." [36]   This, a Greek scholiast comments, is the greatest lie of all !

Now after having seen what a wag Lucian is from his own words, we must decide how we are going to take him. Are we to seek in him relaxation and entertainment (the gift of all true romance) or are we going to marshal our "little learning" to meet his and study all his sources, his parodies of historians and philosophers, or search for allegories in his fantastic worlds ?   The happy way will be along the path of the golden mean.   Gildersleeve put up a

---

[32] I. 4.   The translations of the *True History* are from A. M. Harmon, *Lucian*, I, 247–357 in *The Loeb Classical Library*.

[33] I. 13.
[34] I. 26.
[35] II. 31.
[36] II. 47.

sign-board to it and inscribed directions for future travellers.

"To enjoy the show properly, it is far better for the reader to give himself up to this play of Lucian's fancy than to endeavor to unriddle whatever satire of contemporary literature may lie concealed in its allegory. . . There may be profound meaning in the war which breaks out between the Sunburghers under Phaêthon, and the Moonburghers under Endymion, which begins with the attempt of the Moonburghers to found a colony on the desert planet of Lucifer, and which ends with the victory of the Sunburghers, Lucifer being declared common property and the vanquished compelled to pay an annual tribute of ten thousand *amphoreis* of dew. But so elastic are all such allegories that they can be stretched to fit anything, and the war of these Heliotes and Selenites would answer to describe the conflict between orthodoxy and rationalism, and Lucifer would stand for the coming man. But how much better to look with childish interest on the marshalling of Horsevultures and Chickpeashooters and Garlickfighters and Flea-archers and Windrunners, and to watch the huge spiders spin their web from the moon to Lucifer." [37]

So after realizing that we too may visit the Isles of the Blessed and the Wicked, may soar up to Aristophanes' Cloudcuckooland or dive under the sea in the brother of Jonah's whale, or see Sinbad's roc, let us begin at the beginning. Let the lights go out and the curtain go up. Let us watch breathlessly an ancient Walt Disney fantasy rush across the screen. The very names of countries and peoples add to the excitement as the panorama unrolls. And so vivid are Lucian's descriptions that as in all good movies soon we find ourselves participating in his adventures. Having set out from the Pillars of Hercules with fifty men on a good ship, on the eightieth day we come to a wooded island. Here huge footprints and an inscription reveal that Hercules and Dionysus were here before us. And no wonder, for this is the Isle of Wines : grape-vines produce springs of wine, springs feed rivers, rivers produce

[37] Gildersleeve, *op. cit.*, pp. 318–19.

fish that eaten make people drunk.   And there is a species
of vine that is half grape and half lady like Daphne turning into a laurel and the kiss of the Vine-woman brings
intoxication and her embrace is a prison.   We lost two
of our men to that captivity.

As we set sail, a whirlwind lifted the ship and she became a hydroplane, sailing through the air for seven days
and seven nights.   The island where then we landed
proved to be the Moon.   Endymion is the King so of
course he spoke Greek and we at once joined his forces
for he had a war on with the Men of the Sun, whose King
is Phaethon.   It was all about which should colonize the
Morning Star.   Our fellow Moonites were as strange as
their names : Vulture Knights, Grass Plumes, Pea Shoot-
ers, Garlic Warriors, Flea Bowmen, Wind Aviators, Corn
Sparrows and Crane Knights.   And Phaethon's Heliotes
were as fantastic : Ant Knights, Mosquito Aviators, Dance
Aviators, Stalk Mushrooms, Dog-faced Knights, Cloud
Centaurs.   A fierce battle we had and the Men of the
Sun won because they cut off light from the Moon so
Endymion surrendered.   We saw strange marvels in our
stay on the Moon : how men are the child-bearers ; how
their clothing is made of glass or bronze ; their eyes are
removable ; they have a mirror over a well in which they
can see what happens in far distant lands.

As we voyaged onward, we came to many other countries : to the Morning Star which was just being colonized,
to Lamp Town where among the inhabitants Lucian found
his own Lamp which gave him news of home, to Cloudcuckooland which Aristophanes described so truthfully.
But after such interesting scenes, disaster fell upon us.   A
monstrous whale bore down upon us and in a trice swal-
lowed us, ship and all.

When we recovered from our terror, we found that life

inside a whale is confined but not impossible. We discovered an island where we beached our boat. The whale opened his mouth once an hour so we could mark time and get the points of the compass. And we soon met other men there, a Cypriote called Scintharus and his son. Scintharus told us about the other inhabitants of the whale, who were savage barbarians, and always ready to attack them. We thought best to join Scintharus in subduing these enemies, but the fight was fierce for there were scores of these Lobsters, Crabhands, Tunnyheads, Seagoats, Crawfish Coots and Solefish. After our victory, we lived fairly well in the whale for a year and eight months. In the ninth month, we saw through the teeth of our monster the most terrifying battle, a sea-fight between men riding on huge islands each of which carried about one hundred and twenty.

In spite of seeing such dangers outside, we decided finally that we must escape from our prison. We used fire as a weapon, set the forest at the tail-end aflame and after twelve days found that the whale was going to die. Just in time we propped open his mouth with huge beams and the next day when he expired, out we went on our good ship and felt once more the wind in our sails. Fair weather did not last long. A terrible northern gale descended and froze all the sea to a depth of six fathoms. Scintharus, who was now our ship-master, saved us by directing us to excavate a cave-home in the ice. In it we lived for thirty days, building a fire and cooking the fish we cut out of the ice. When food gave out, we dug out the boat and sailed over the ice as though it were the sea until on the fifth day we came to open water. Now we kept coming to various islands. We got water at one and at the next one milk, for this island had grapes whose juice was milk, and its earth was cheese. It was easy to

subsist there !   Next we passed the Isle of Cork where the
city is built on a cork foundation and the men have feet
of cork so that they can run over the waters as they will,
buoyed up by their own life-preservers !

Happiest of all our stays was that on the Island of the
Blessed.   Here it is always spring.   Every month the vines
yield grapes and the trees fruit.   It is a land flowing with
milk and wine.   Glass trees furnish goblets which fill
automatically at the banquet.   Baked loaves of bread are
plucked from trees.   Beside the table are two springs,
one of laughter, one of joy, and with draughts from these
the banqueters start their revels.   Famous men dwell
there.   I saw Socrates surrounded by fair young men argu-
ing with Nestor and Palamedes.   Plato preferred to live
in his own Republic.   The followers of Aristippus and
Epicurus were considered the best of companions, but
Diogenes the Cynic had reformed, married Lais and taken
to dancing.   The Stoics had not yet arrived for they were
still toiling up the steep hill of virtue.   Conversation with
Homer was one of the greatest pleasures, especially as he
settled the matter of his birthplace by declaring himself
a Babylonian and solved the Homeric question by affirm-
ing that he had written all the lines attributed to him.
Beside literary talks, there were games for the Dead.

Even the Island of the Blessed could not be free from
wars, for the Wicked invaded it and had to be expelled by
force.   Homer wrote a new epic on the fight of the dead
heroes.   The Island had its scandals too all due again to
Helen.   For she bewitched Scintharus' son and tried to
elope with him, but was caught.   That episode caused our
expulsion from the Island of the Blessed.   Before we left,
Homer wrote a couplet for Lucian which he had carved on
a stele of beryl and Odysseus secretly gave him a letter
for Calypso.

We touched at the Isle of the Wicked and at the Isle of Dreams, where we slept thirty days and next we put in at Ogygia.   Lucian read Odysseus' letter before he delivered it to Calypso and found he had always regretted leaving her !   For Odysseus' sake, Calypso entertained us royally.

Next we fell into danger from the Pumpkin Pirates and the Hardshell Pirates and the Dolphin-Riders, but we escaped them all.   One night we ran aground on the marvellous and mighty nest of a king-fisher.   And a little further on in the sea we came to a forest of rootless trees which we could not penetrate.   There was nothing to do but haul the ship up to their tops and take "a forest cruise" across.   More marvellous still we had to cross a water-chasm on a water bridge, a river-way between two water precipices.   After that we came to the Isle of the Bellowing Bullheads, men like Minotaurs, and had some skirmishes with them.   And then we came to an Island of Fair Ladies who wished to take us to bed with them, but Lucian discovered that they all had ass-legs and that they ate strangers when they had cozened them to sleep.   So we departed in haste.   At dawn we saw the land which is on the other side of the world from ours and there we were shipwrecked.   What happened there will be another story.

This review of the two books of Lucian's *True History* reveals at once its startling differences from the other Greek romances of the early Empire.   Romantic love does not figure in it.   Religion has little or no place in it.   Adventures are its bones and sinews.   These adventures though described realistically are all figments of the imagination, explorations of the Wonderful Things beyond Thule as much as those of Antonius Diogenes must have been.   The coloring of the pictures is an amazing mixture

of realism and fantasy. The veracity of sense impressions
almost converts doubting Thomases. Lucian comes to
seem no mean rival of Herodotus, the Father of Lies. Only
occasionally some satiric laughter betrays him.

It is perhaps easier for twentieth century readers to accept his wonders than it was for his contemporaries of
the second century. Science has developed so many
of his imaginative forecasts. The monstrous footprints of
Hercules and Dionysus might be rock-prints of dinosaurs.
The plunging whale is a submarine. His ship lifting from
the ocean to sail through the air has become the hydroplane. His island galleys bearing one hundred and twenty
men each are our battleships. The Cloud Centaurs who
fight in the air are our aviators. Arctic explorers have
lived in huts made of ice-blocks. Ice-sailing is a recognized winter sport. Clothing is made not of glass or
bronze, but of cellulose and steel. Removable eyes suggest spectacles, contact lenses and field-glasses. The Cork-
footed Men must have resembled surf riders. And the
magic mirror over the well anticipated the perforated
sphere of television.

But his contemporaries had the advantage of us in recognizing Lucian's sources and parodies more readily than we
can. For us, Antonius Diogenes, Ctesias and Iambulus
are lost. Yet Photius records that the romance of Antonius Diogenes, *The Wonders beyond Thule,* was the
chief source of Lucian's *True History.* So many, however, are the sources which Lucian used to forward his
avowed purpose of furnishing relaxation accompanied by
some learning, that scholars have busied themselves for
years tracing parallels with Greek and Latin authors.[38]

[38] See E. Rohde, *Der Griechische Roman,* Leipzig, 1914, pp. 204–209 ; 242–
50, 260 ff. ; C. S. Jerram, *Luciani Vera Historia,* Oxford, 1887, I, 120 and *passim* ;
H. W. L. Hime, *Lucian the Syrian Satirist,* London, 1900, app. pp. 91–95 ; F. W.
Householder, Jr., *Literary Quotation and Allusion in Lucian,* New York, 1941.

Allinson remarks wisely : "In general, it seems safe to con-
clude that Lucian regarded the writings of predecessors
and contemporaries as an open quarry from which he first
built up his own style and then picked out material to
imbed, with an artist's skill, in the parti-coloured mosaic
of his satire." [39]

Some idea of Lucian's parody of his sources may be
gained, even though Antonius Diogenes is lost, from his
incidental flings at great Greeks and from his constant
references to Homer which are a mixture of admiration
and irony. So when he saw Cloudcuckooland he re-
membered Aristophanes the poet, "a wise and truth-
ful man whose writings are distrusted without reason." [40]
On the Island of the Blessed he did not find Plato for he
preferred to live in the city of his imagination under his
own constitution and laws. Yet he might well have been
in Elysium for the inhabitants are most Platonic in sharing
their wives.[41] The solemn treaty which ended the wars
between the Men of the Sun and the Men of the Moon has
a comical resemblance to the treaty between Athens and
Sparta which Thucydides records though it is signed by
Fireman, Hotman, and Burner, by Nightman, Moonman
and Allbright.[42]

Herodotus comes in for more imitation, for he furnishes
stories of ants bigger than foxes,[43] of dog-headed men,[44]
of men who feed on odors,[45] of a feast of lanterns in Egypt,[46]
of a floating island,[47] of the sea freezing,[48] of a breeze that
bears the perfume of Arabia.[49] But when Lucian solemnly imitates these exaggerations, we feel he has his
tongue in his cheek and our suspicion is confirmed when

[39] F. G. Allinson, *Lucian Satirist
and Artist,* Boston, 1926, p. 123.
[40] I. 29.
[41] II. 17 and 19.
[42] I. 20, Thuc. V. 18.
[43] I. 16, Her. III. 102.
[44] I. 16, Her. IV. 191.
[45] I. 23, Her. I. 202 ; IV. 75.
[46] I. 29, Her. II. 62.
[47] I. 40, Her. II. 156.
[48] II. 2, Her. IV. 28.
[49] II. 5, Her. III. 113.

he consigns Ctesias and Herodotus to the limbo of Liars in the Island of the Wicked.[50]

Lucian's treatment of Homer shows his most genial irony. In his preface he makes Homer's Odysseus the guide and teacher of all historians of imaginary travels, Odysseus "who tells Alcinous and his court about winds in bondage, one-eyed men, cannibals and savages ; also about animals with many heads, and transformations of his comrades wrought with drugs," and with such marvels "humbugged the illiterate Phaeacians." [51] But in the Island of the Blessed, Homer is the shade in whose talk Lucian most delights. Homer indeed is most affable in discussing all the literary problems of his epics, especially since he had just won a lawsuit in which Thersites accused him of libel, through the aid of his lawyer Odysseus.[52] Homer as a shade is still writing for when there was war in heaven, he produced a new epic about the battle of the shades of the heroes,[53] which Lucian unfortunately lost on the way home, and on Lucian's departure Homer composed a commemorative epigram which described him as dear to the blessed gods.[54]

Lucian introduces Homer's characters into his scenes. Achilles is one of the most honored heroes on the Island of the Blessed, serving as joint judge with Theseus at the Games of the Dead.[55] Helen is the leading lady in the court-room scene where Rhadamanthus had to decide whose wife she should be in Elysium. She has forgiven Stesichorus for saying she caused the Trojan War.[56] But she creates a new scandal by trying to desert Menelaus again in an elopement with Scintharus' son.[57] Calypso on receiving Odysseus' letter from Lucian's hand weeps

50 II. 31.
51 I. 3.
52 II. 20.
53 II. 24.
54 II. 28.
55 II. 22.
56 II. 15.
57 II. 25–26.

as she reads that he always regretted giving up his life with her, and then with true feminine curiosity asks how Penelope is looking now and whether she is as wise as Odysseus used to boast. Lucian made such replies as he thought would gratify her ! [58]

Minor episodes are reminiscent of the Odyssey. Rhadamanthus gives Lucian a talisman of mallow as Hermes gave Odysseus the moly.[59] To the Land of Dreams Lucian must erect four gates in place of Homer's two, one of horn, one of ivory.[60] And the Singing Sirens that tried to beguile Odysseus have been metamorphosed into fair young ladies in long chitons which conceal the legs of she-asses.[61] But whatever changes are made in the source-material taken from the Odyssey, Lucian's gentle raillery does not hide his admiration of great Homer. He gives the lie to the myth that Homer was blind.[62] And in the contest of the poets at the Games of the Dead in the Island of the Blessed, he ironically makes Hesiod the victor though he affirms that in truth Homer was by far the best of poets.

Lucian's style in his *True History* illustrates many of his own criteria for writing history. The short preface is in proportion to the short two-book *True History*. The narrative is concise, rapid, lucid and shows consistent progress, one event following naturally and quickly upon another without extravagant use of details. The few speeches are short, lively and suited to the character of the speaker. The descriptions are realistic and pointed. Extraordinary stories are told simply with an appearance of veracity.

A few typical elements of the Greek Romances appear in the *True History*. There is a suggestion of a court-room

[58] II. 35–36.
[59] II. 28, *Odys.* X. 302–306.
[60] II. 33, *Odys.* XIX. 562–67.

[61] II. 46, *Odys.* XII. 37–200.
[62] II. 20.

scene where Rhadamanthus judges Helen's accomplices in escape. One letter is inserted, Odysseus' to Calypso, for the purpose of ironic satire of Homeric characters. An inscription on bronze is discovered and a laudatory couplet in hexameter is composed and inscribed on stone. But love and religion, the commonest themes of the Greek Romances, are eliminated from this tale of marvellous adventures.

Satire though this story is, it ranks easily first among imaginary voyagings both in fantasy and style. In his narration Lucian pours all his spirit, his liveliness of observation, his brilliant imagination, his vivacious wit. His own enjoyment in his facile, marvellous inventions is contagious. As he rushes his breathless readers over the earth, through the air, under the sea, as he introduces us to innumerable natural phenomena and monstrous beings, he convinces us that this world of fantasy is a real world. He has made many others wish to record similar travels, for the *True History* is the model of all those imaginary voyages with which Rabelais, Cyrano de Bergerac, Swift, Voltaire and others amused their contemporaries. No work of Lucian found so many imitators as this.[63]

The readers of Lucian's *True History* on finishing it feel that they have drunk with him more from his eternal springs of joy and laughter than from his irony, in fact that his irony gives only a few drops of angostura bitters to the heady cocktails of his wit. And at the end the readers of this romance are ready today to salute the shade of Lucian as Andrew Lang did : [64]

"In what bower, oh Lucian, of your rediscovered Islands Fortunate are you now reclining ; the delight of the fair, the learned, the witty, and the brave ? . . .

[63] See M. Croiset, *op. cit.*, C. XII, "La fantaisie chez Lucien" ; and F. G. Allinson, *op. cit.*, *passim*.

[64] Andrew Lang, *Letters to Dead Authors*, New York, 1893, pp. 53–54.

"There, among the vines that bear twelve times in the year, more excellent than all the vineyards of Touraine, while the song-birds bring you flowers from vales enchanted, and the shapes of the Blessed come and go, beautiful in wind-woven raiment of sunset hues ; there, in a land that knows not age, nor winter, midnight, nor autumn, nor noon, where the silver twilight of summer-dawn is perennial, where youth does not wax spectre-pale and die ; there, my Lucian, you are crowned the Prince of the Paradise of Mirth."

It may seem anti-climax to turn from the *True History* to Lucian's other romance, the *Metamorphoses,* for the second exists only in an epitome by another hand. Since however this epitome is included in all the best manuscripts and has been proved conclusively by B. E. Perry to be a condensation of an original *Metamorphoses* by Lucian on the basis of spirit, vocabulary, syntax and phraseology, we must try to form some idea of this other romance.[65]

As the *True History* is a satire of travellers' tales, this epitome, *Lucius or Ass,* is primarily a satire of magic and magic rites. Just as in the *True History* not only epic poets and historians were parodied, but philosophers came in for their share of ironic comment, so in *Lucius or Ass* satire is directed not merely against magicians, but also against corrupt priests and frail women. The satire is of the earth, earthy, very near the folk-story from which it may have originated. *Lucius or Ass* is Everyman in his credulity, gullibility and bestiality. The only heroines in his murky world are a witch-woman and a corrupt maid. This epitome has two great values : it gives us some idea of Lucian's lost *Metamorphoses,* and hence affords a basis for comparison with Apuleius' great Latin novel *Metamorphoses.* It will prove convenient I hope, to have a rather full outline presented here in English for purposes of dis-

[65] Ben Edwin Perry, *The Metamorphoses Ascribed to Lucius of Patrae,* Princeton, 1920.

cussion and comparison.   This Greek *Lucius or Ass* like
the *True History* is written in the first person, but Lucius
of Patrae, the hero, not the author, is the narrator.   In my
brief résumé, I have found it clearer to write Lucius' account in the third person.

Once upon a time on a journey to Thessaly Lucius in-
quires of some fellow travellers whereabouts in the city of
Hypata a man named Hipparchus lives, for he is carrying
a letter of introduction to him.   On his arrival he stays at
Hipparchus' house.   Only his wife and a maid Palaestra
lived with him.   On his host's inquiring the object of his
travels, Lucius says he is on his way to Larissa.   He conceals
the fact that he is searching for women who deal in magic.
While walking around the city, he meets an old friend of
his mother named Abroea, who warns him against the wife
of Hipparchus because she is a witch.   Lucius, delighted
with this news, returns to Hipparchus' house and in the
absence of his host and hostess makes love to Palaestra with
the purpose of persuading the maid to acquaint him with
her mistress' magic powers.   At the close of a night of
revel, Lucius persuades Palaestra to show him her mistress
at her magic rites.

A few nights later Palaestra fulfills her promise by leading Lucius at dead of night to the door of her lady's bed-
room where through a crack he can watch her proceedings.
She mutters to her lamp.   She strips.   She rubs her naked
body with ointment from a little box.   Gradually she is
transformed into an owl and flies away to her lover.   Lucius then prevails upon Palaestra to let him attempt the
same transformation.   By ill luck the maid brings him
the wrong box of ointment so that he is changed not into
a bird, but into an ass.   Palaestra soothingly assures him
that the antidote is simple, just a meal of roses, and if her

dearest will pass the night quietly in the stable, in the morning she will gather the flowers and recover her Lucius.

But this simple plan gangs a-gley, for in the night robbers raid the house, secure much booty and to carry it steal also the horse and the real ass of Hipparchus and Lucius. So the man-ass, heavily burdened, is driven to the robbers' home. One old woman is their care-taker. Several days later the robbers return from one of their forays bringing in as booty a young woman whom they have kidnapped. Later on in the absence of the brigands the girl tries to escape riding on the ass, but both are captured by the robbers. On their return, they find that the old woman in terror has hanged herself.

The robbers plan a dreadful punishment for the culprits : to kill the ass, disembowel him and sew the girl up alive in his paunch to die by slow torture. But before they achieve this horror, a company of soldiers arrives, captures the whole band and carries them off to a magistrate. They had been conducted to the robbers' den by the fiancé of the girl. He now escorts her home on the honored ass Lucius.

After the wedding of the happy pair, the bride persuades her father to reward the ass her benefactor so he is to be turned out into pasture with the she-asses. But the servant to whom the care of the ass is intrusted wickedly takes him home and makes him labor first in a mill, then carrying fagots on a steep mountain, where a cruel driver mistreats him. In the midst of his sufferings, news comes that the bride and groom have been drowned on the seashore. So since their new masters are dead, the servants all flee, taking the ass with them. They sell him in a city of Macedonia to a eunuch priest of a Syrian goddess. In his life with the priests, Lucius is so horrified by their im-

pure practices that he brays loudly in protest. The noise
brings up some passing peasants who go off to tell the
village the obscenities they have witnessed. The priests
have to flee for their lives, but first they nearly kill the ass
by beating him for his braying.

Lucius is in danger of his life again at the house of a rich
man where they stop. For the servants who have lost the
meat of a wild ass which was to be the dinner (the dogs
stole it), plot to kill Lucius and serve up his flesh. He
saves himself only by running away from the cook. The
priests are now arrested because they are found in possession of a golden phiale which they stole from a temple,
and the ass is sold to a baker. In the mill Lucius is so
worn down by the hard work that he is sold as worthless to
an old gardener. On the way to town, this gardener has
a quarrel with a soldier and nearly kills him so the gardener and the ass have to go into hiding. Stupid Lucius
betrays their hiding place by putting his head out of an
upper window to see what is going on. Captured he is
given to the soldier, but he soon sells him to a cook. Now
Lucius fattens on good food by surreptitious filching of
choice portions which the cook and his brother had re-
served for themselves. By a little detective work the
brothers discover that the thief is the ass. They show him
eating men's food to their master, who promptly buys the
ass, has a servant train him to act like a man (easy lessons
for Lucius !) and exhibits him for admission fees. A
woman buys a night with him and has intercourse with
him.

Then his master purposes to exhibit him couched with
a woman (a condemned criminal) at a public festival.
The scene is all set when some one comes up to Lucius and
the woman at the banquet table bearing, among other
flowers, roses. At last the ass has his meal of restorative

flowers and becomes once more Lucius. He appeals to
the magistrate for protection against those who cry he is
a magician and must be killed. He informs the governor
that his name is Lucius, he has a brother Gaius, both have
the same two other names ; that he himself is a writer of
stories and his brother is an elegiac poet and a good
prophet. The magistrate believing his story gives him
hospitality. Lucius' brother comes to take him home,
but first Lucius thought it fitting to call on the woman
who had given him her love when he was an ass. He is
chagrined to find that as a man he has no charm for her !
He sails with his brother to Patrae and there sacrifices to
the gods who have saved him.

No other work attributed to Lucian has aroused greater
controversy than *Lucius or Ass*. All the literature about
it is reviewed in Ben Edwin Perry's epoch-making book
The Metamorphoses Ascribed to Lucius of Patrae, which
conclusively proves that *Lucius or Ass* is an epitome of
Lucian's *Metamorphoses,* made by another writer. Perry
analyzes Photius' description of the lost Greek *Metamorphoses* with its theory of the three versions of the ass-
story,[66] and proves that Photius' one mistake was in thinking that the name Lucius of Patrae referred to an author of
a third *Metamorphoses,* which was probably the original
of Lucian's and Apuleius' stories : Lucius of Patrae in
Lucius or Ass is the hero-narrator, not the author. Perry
then with convincing logic reconstructs the probable content of the *Metamorphoses* of which *Lucius or Ass* is an
epitome and with the same irrefutable reasoning discusses
the nature of this original Greek novel. The basis of it
was a folk-lore story of a transformation. The style was
plain, the narrative rapid, the tone ironic. The narrator
keeps the character of the hero of the adventures and never

[66] *Bibl. Cod.* 129, Migne.

identifies himself with the author.   The character of the hero is that of "an unique clown" with an absorbing and credulous interest in strange phenomena especially transformations.   The final proof that the *Metamorphoses* was satirical is "the simple fact that the *Eselmensch* is a litterateur and an investigator of marvels."   "The generic title shows that the author regarded his story as a kind of commentary on the subject of metamorphoses, and writers who interested themselves in such things." [67]

This author, "second century Atticist, humorist, and satirist," can be none other than Lucian himself, for the Greek *Metamorphoses* is Lucianic in type, is a relaxation from serious work as is the *True History* ; it shows the same satire of credulity that other works of Lucian (for example the *Alexander*) did ; and it is colored by the same ironic humor.   The epitome contains a striking Lucianic element although this is overlaid by philological errors. Perry also analyzes resemblances and differences between the reconstructed *Metamorphoses* of Lucian and Apuleius' novel, but this discussion I shall reserve for the next chapter.

Lucius or Ass is valuable in proving that Lucian wrote not one but two romances ; that in both he developed a new type of romance, the satiric ; that in each he maintained the same great qualities which mark his other writings : the quest for truth, intolerance of fraud and credulity ; keen observation and realistic description ; condensation, rapidity, clarity ; dramatic irony.   The two romances also show more than any other of Lucian's writings his brilliant imaginative powers.

A postscript to this discussion of Lucian's satiric romances may well include an account of a novel in miniature which appears in one of his dialogues.   Writing in

[67] B. E. Perry, *op. cit.,* pp. 52–55.

the second century he was of course thoroughly familiar with the conventional type of the Greek romance.
Though this statement might be accepted *a priori*, certain
evidence of it is furnished by his insertion in his *Toxaris*
of an epitome of a Scythian romance of love and adventure.
The *Toxaris* is a Platonic dialogue written probably about
A.D. 165, in Lucian's period of transition from purely
rhetorical writings to those of moral or religious satire.[68]
In it a Greek Mnesippus and a Scythian Toxaris discuss
friendship each giving five illustrations of famous in-
stances in his own country. The longest one related is a
Scythian romance told by Toxaris.[69] Rostovtzeff has
shown that Lucian probably had in his hands a Greek
romance with a Scythian background, for papyri fragments furnish incontrovertible evidence of a similar Scythian romance in Greek dating from the second century
A.D.[70]

The story as told by Lucian is melodramatic. It relates
the devotion of three Scythians, Macentes, Lonchates and
Arsacomas, who had pledged to each other friendship for
life and death in the old Scythian way of shedding some of
their blood into a cup and quaffing it to-gether. Now
Arsacomas, who had gone on a mission to Leucanor, king
of Bosporus, there fell madly in love at first sight with his
daughter Mazaea. At a banquet when suitors were bid-
ding for the hand of the princess with proud lists of their
possessions, all Arsacomas could boast of was his two fair,
brave friends. The Bosporans laughed him to scorn and
the girl was awarded to Adyrmachus, who the next day
was to convey his bride to the land of the Machlyans.

[68] M. Croiset, *op. cit.*, p. 48.

[69] Harmon, *op. cit.*, V, 101–207.

[70] M. Rostovtzeff, *Seminarium
Kondakovianum*, II, 135–38, Prague,
1928 ; *Papyri Greci e Latini*, VIII. No.

981. For a different point of view see
F. Zimmermann, "Lukians Toxaris
und das Kairener Romanfragment"
in *Philologische Wochenschrift*, 55
(1935), 1211–16.

The outraged Arsacomas rushing home told his friends how he and their friendship had been ridiculed and the three as one man planned immediate vengeance. Lonchates promised to bring Arsacomas the head of Leucanor. Macentes was to kidnap the bride. Arsacomas was to stay at home and raise an army on the ox-hide for the war that would surely follow. All proceeded according to schedule. Arsacomas slew an ox, cut up and cooked the meat, spread the hide on the ground and sat on it with his hands held behind him. This is the greatest appeal for aid possible for a man who desires to secure help for vengeance. His friends and kinsmen coming accepted each a portion of the meat, set right foot on the hide and pledged as much aid as he could. So a goodly army was raised.

Lonchates went to Bosporus, pretending he had come as a friend to offer aid against Arsacomas' planned invasion. King Leucanor alarmed by the news of an imminent Scythian attack was lured alone into the temple of Ares to take a secret oath of friendship with Lonchates. There Lonchates murdered him, cut off his head and escaped with it under his cloak before the guards outside knew what had happened.

Macentes too used subterfuge, for hurrying to the Machlyans he reported King Leucanor's death, said falsely that the Bosporans called Adyrmachus as his son-in-law to be their king, and offered while Adyrmachus rode at full speed to them, to escort after him his bride Mazaea in the wagon-train, for she, he claimed, was a relative of his own. This plan worked so smoothly that Macentes, when night came on, took Mazaea from her carriage, put her on his horse with himself and galloped off with her to Arsacomas. The horse dropped dead at the end but the kidnapped bride was delivered. Then all three friends united in the battle against Adyrmachus, slew him on the field, and by nightfall had won a victory. The next day peace was negotiated. Such are the deeds of daring which Scythians perform for their friends.

In the papyrus fragments a lady in distress is weeping and lamenting in the tent of a general Eubiotus. He clears his tent because of her woe, hears her declare that she wishes she had never seen Eraseinus (apparently her lover) and prevents her attempted suicide by wresting her sword from her. She then tells Eubiotus that she is not the Amazon Themisto though she is so disguised, but a Greek girl Calligone. Here the fragments end. The only points in common with Lucian's story are the geographical background and the name Eubiotus (in Lucian the illegitimate brother of Leucanor and an aspirant to his throne),[71] but both stories as Rostovtzeff points out look to history for characters and setting as the Ninus Romance did.

In the *Toxaris* the coloring is only quasi-historical through the mention of names of kings and their lineage : the story is not history, but an historical novel. And the connection of the Scythians with the Sarmatians, the Alans, the Maeotians and the Bosporans corresponds only in part with their actual relations at the time. The Sauromatians are a relic of the past ; the Alans represent actual conditions in the time of the author. The geographical coloring is likewise only partly historical. The picture of the Scythians even with its tendency to idealization represents the people fairly. They are nomadic, poor, with a free democratic political organization without kings, and they are warriors. Their gods are the sword and the wind. Their customs are primitive. They make war on their neighbors and have special relations with the Greek states

---

[71] R. M. Rattenbury, "Romance : the Greek Novel" in *New Chapters in the History of Greek Literature, Third Series*, pp. 240–44.

on the Bosporus and Olbia and visit those on the south side
of the Black Sea.

Lucian in composing his *Toxaris* probably had in hand
a Greek romance with a Scythian background, containing
certain historical and ethnographical material. This he
worked over making his story represent what his public
then knew or could know of the Scythians and their neighbors. The discovery of the papyrus fragments of the Calligone novel confirms this thesis.[72] The type of the *Toxaris* story and the papyrus story is the same. Both were
love romances, though in each the erotic motif is subordi-
nated to adventure. The interest of the age in the unfamiliar, the strange is manifested in the selection of
Scythia for the background.

Lucian's narrative is intensely exciting as well as picturesque and although it is only a miniature story it gives
us an idea of another love romance of a wild type with a
king's head cut off for vengeance, a bride kidnapped on
horseback and an army raised on the ox-hide. The whole
Toxaris indeed, as Croiset remarked,[73] with its ten anecdotes furnishes rich examples of Lucian's art of narration.

[72] M. Rostovtzeff, *Scythien und der*   [73] M. Croiset, *op. cit.*, p. 51.
Bosporus, Berlin, 1931, I, 96–99.

VIII

A COMPARISON OF THE GREEK ROMANCES AND APULEIUS' METAMORPHOSES

APULEIUS, the author of the greatest ancient novel extant, might, if he had chosen, written his book in Greek instead of Latin. Though he was born in North Africa (at Madaura) he was educated in Athens as well as Roman Carthage and Rome, indeed was completely bi-lingual. The letter from his wife produced as evidence in his trial for having won her affections by magic was in Greek. And private correspondence demonstrates fluency in the language even more than does the fact of his translation of a work by Plato and his Latin style richly colored by Greek syntax and vocabulary.

Some reader may now ask as Apuleius anticipated: "Who is this man?"[1] So I must refer all to my other writings about him and briefly characterize him here for the uninformed.[2] Apuleius was born about A.D. 125 in the Roman colony of Madaura where his father was a leading citizen and official. He was educated at Carthage, Athens and Rome, was certainly bi-lingual and probably tri-lingual as he must have known Punic as well as Latin

[1] Quis ille ? *Met.* I. 1.
[2] E. H. Haight, *Apuleius and his Influence*, New York, 1927; "The Myth of Cupid and Psyche in Ancient Art" in *Art and Archaeology*, III (1916), 43-52, 87-97; "The Myth of Cupid and Psyche in Renaissance Art," "The Vassar College Psyche Tapestries," in *Art and Archaeology*, XV (1923), 107–116; "Apuleius' Art of Story-Telling" in *Essays on Ancient Fiction*, New York, 1936.

and Greek.   Returning to Africa, he practiced success-
fully the art of a sophist, giving public discourses, many of
them impromptu.   Specimens of these are extant in a collection of extracts from his speeches called the *Florida*.
He married a wealthy widow, mother of a university friend
at Athens, and was promptly sued by his in-laws for having
gained her hand by magic practices.   The brilliant speech
in which he defended himself at Sabrata against their
charges, the *Apologia,* is extant and constitutes his autobiography.   St. Augustine called him a Platonist and he did
indeed try to convey Plato's ideas to his contemporaries in
works on *The God of Socrates, Plato and his Doctrine* and
other lost writings.   His fame when he was alive rested
on his oratory and it was so great that he was honored by
statues and made priest of Aesculapius at Carthage.   But
his undying glory comes from his novel, the *Metamorphoses*.   The date of its composition is uncertain as indeed
are most of the dates of his life.   He lived from about A.D.
125 to A.D. 171, that is, in the time of Antoninus Pius and
Marcus Aurelius.   He was therefore a contemporary of
Lucian and may have met him as Walter Pater imagines in
Marius the Epicurean.   What concerns us here is his novel
and its relation to the Greek Romances.

The *Metamorphoses* of Apuleius is a long story written
in eleven books.   It is an ego-romance with Lucius a Greek
acting as narrator and hero.

"The plot is simple.   The hero Lucius who is greatly interested
in magic is enabled by the aid of the maid-servant of a witch to
achieve transformation.   But a mistake in the use of the unguents
changes him not into a bird as he had planned, but into an ass.
Although he knows that the antidote is a meal of roses, he is kept by
Fortune from securing release through long months and meets various adventures until at last through the aid of the goddess Isis
Lucius the Ass becomes again Lucius the Man." [8]

[8] From E. H. Haight, "Apuleius' Art of Story-Telling," in *Essays on Ancient
Fiction*, New York, 1936, p. 152.

The similarity of this plot to that of the Greek *Lucius or Ass* is apparent at once. But its unique differences caused by diversification of anecdotes and long additions become clear as we read the narrative.

Lucius in the beginning was travelling in Thessaly riding his white horse over the high mountains when he fell in with two other travellers. One of these as they rode on together related a horrible story of how his friend Socrates saw a companion murdered by a witch. The scene of the story was set in Hypata, the very city to which Lucius was going. And the narrative of it by its effect on Lucius reveals all his credulity and curiosity about witchcraft.

Lucius was entertained at the house of Milo to whom he brought a letter of introduction and soon he learned from a relative in Hypata, named Byrrhaena, that Milo's wife Pamphile was a witch. Hypata was full of stories of marvellous happenings and soon Lucius heard another of these thrillers at a dinner-party given by Byrrhaena. It was the story told by a guest Tlelyphron of how he watched a corpse for pay and thereby suffered mutilation of his face by a foul beldam. It was on the way home from the party that Lucius, jittery and drunk, fought his fatal battle with three bold robbers who afterwards, at his trial for murder at the Festival of Risus, god of laughter, were proved to be wine-skins !

Now Lucius was determined to investigate magic rites by personal experience so he made ardent love to Pamphile's servant Fotis until the enamored girl consented to let him peer through a crack in the door of Pamphile's bed-room and see her mistress transform herself into an owl. This marvel witnessed, nothing would satisfy Lucius but to attempt a similar transformation. Unfortunately Fotis gave him the wrong unguent for the necessary lubrication of his body and he became not a bird, but an

ass ! The careless maid swore that the antidote was simple, merely a meal of roses, and if he would quietly spend
the night in the stable, in the morning she would bring
him a breakfast of the flowers. Unfortunately before
dawn robbers arrived, pillaged the house and stole, along
with Lucius' own horse and Milo's ass, Lucius the ass to
carry the plunder. This was the beginning of a long
series of adventures for the man-ass before he could achieve
re-transformation.

In the robbers' hide-out in the mountains Lucius heard
the robbers tell three fine stories of their brave chieftains.
There too he saw a band of robbers bring in a captive
beauty Charite and heard her piteous tale of how she was
kidnapped on her wedding-night for ransom. To cheer
this weeping girl the old woman who cooked for the robbers told in their absence the story of Cupid and Psyche.

An old wives' tale she called it, but Apuleius lifted the
folk-tale to the realm of the Olympian gods by making it
the love romance of Venus' son Cupid and Psyche, a mortal maid. Venus herself was the cruel step-mother who
tried to separate the lovers and set all sorts of impossible
tasks for Psyche. But the heroine triumphed over every
task by the aid of Cupid's minions on earth and in air. Finally the king of heaven, Jupiter himself, called Psyche to
his high throne to receive the gift of immortality and
summoned all the great gods and goddesses to celebrate
her nuptials with the god of love himself.

This happy love romance diverted Charite only briefly,
but soon her lover disguised as a robber came and rescued
her and after causing the destruction of all the robber band
carried her away with Lucius to safety. Charite's story,
however, unlike Psyche's was not to end happily. For
after her marriage to her Tlepolemus, a former suitor
Thrasyllus because of jealousy made way with her hus-

band in a boar hunt, pretending his death was an accident. Later when the villain was making ardent love to the widow, the shade of her husband appeared and recounted his murder at the hands of his friend. Charite by subtle plans was able to put out Thrasyllus' eyes for vengeance and then stabbed herself over her husband's tomb. Thrasyllus in repentance starved himself to death.

Lucius the Ass again left to the mercy of Fortune had a series of degrading adventures which tended to make him a pessimist. He witnessed the obscene orgies of a lewd band of Syrian priests. He heard four naughty Milesian Tales of corrupt women : "The Lover under the Tub," "The Baker's Wife," "The Sandals under the Bed," "The Fuller's Wife." These Milesian Tales of triangular sex episodes are succeeded in the novel by another group of tragic stories which stir deeper waters. The first is a record of the terrible oppression of the poor by an arrogant young nobleman and how three fine young brothers who went to the defense of the poor family lost their lives in a noble cause. Then follows a tragic story of an amorous step-mother and her attempt to poison her unresponsive step-son. And finally comes the awful narrative of five murders committed by one sadistic woman. Book Ten concludes with the plan to display Lucius the ass in obscene union with this condemned criminal at a public exhibition. To avoid this horror, Lucius ran away from Corinth to the sea-shore at Cenchreae and there found his salvation.

For lying asleep on the sea-shore that night he had a vision in the moonlight of the goddess Isis. In all her refulgent beauty she told him of herself and gave him hope. For she assured him that at the spring festival of the launching of her sacred vessel she would give him certain aid. And indeed it was at that festival in the midst of all its brilliant pageantry that the priest of Isis offered the ass a garland of roses and munching them he became man again. No wonder that after that Lucius had only one desire : to serve his savior.

Night after night he had new visions of the goddess and under the direction of her priest he fulfilled all the arduous preparations for the initiation into her rites. Finally one night left alone in her temple he was vouchsafed that mystic experience which only the elect may achieve, death, rebirth, revelation.

"I approached the borderland of death, trod the threshold of Proserpina, was borne through all the elements and returned ; at midnight I saw the sun shining with a brilliant light ; I approached the gods of the nether and the upper world and adored them in person near at hand." [4]

After such exaltation Lucius consecrated himself forever to the service of Isis. Soon going to Rome he continued his worship at her temple there and by her direction was twice initiated into the mysteries of the god Osiris though the expense was great for "this poor man of Madaura." Under the blessing of Osiris he prospered greatly as an advocate in the Roman Forum and finally under the god's direction he was allowed to become one of the Pastophores or high-priests of the cult. So ends his metamorphosis and the novel.

Let us now return to the beginning. In the first chapter Apuleius announced that he is telling a Greek story. The main outline of his plot is indeed identical with that of the Greek *Lucius or Ass*, which as we have seen, is an epitome of the Greek *Metamorphoses* by Lucian. Apuleius' novel is clearly later than Lucian's because of rich and notable additions to the plot of the epitome *Lucius or Ass*. These additions are Milesian Tales, the Cupid and

4 *Met.* XI, 23.

Psyche story and the great eleventh book portraying the worship of Isis, who redeemed Lucius from ass to human shape.

The change in the tone of telling the whole story is significant for while the earthy character of the original folktale occasionally appears and there are recurrent glimpses of Lucianic wit and satire, Apuleius' *Metamorphoses* is neither a comic romance nor a satire as Lucian's clearly was. Apuleius wrote a serious novel, a sort of Pilgrim's Progress of the Ass-Man in his quest for knowledge of marvels. Whereas Lucian through satire degraded a simple folk-tale, Apuleius exalted it by making the journeyings of Lucius a search for the spiritual meaning of life. His hero walks alone. The love romance in his story, the Cupid and Psyche tale, starts with the Platonic conception of the relation of Eros and Psyche, Love and the Soul, and therefrom is lifted to the realm of the Olympian gods. And finally the retransformation of Lucius is no chance event, but a salvation wrought out by the mystic worship of Isis.

The subjectivity infused in the plot by these additions is enhanced by the fact that the hero-narrator Lucius is identified with the author, implicitly at first in the Preface and in incidental comment of author to reader ; in the last book by the identification of Lucius with "the poor man of Madaura" so that the whole narrative becomes personal experience. This fact involves another difference from the structure of the Greek love romances. The action of these love romances, as Riefstahl points out,[5] is a "closed" one : in the misfortunes which threaten the lovers through Fortune, they must always remain faithful to each other and stout-hearted in order to be re-united. So the circle

[5] Hermann Riefstahl, *Der Roman des Apuleius*, Frankfurt am Main, 1938, pp. 83–84.

of the action is "closed," for it is a great cycle in the life
of the hero which places him at the end just where he was
in the beginning.   The action in Apuleius is "open," for
the hero is bound and pledged to nothing.   He goes
through his adventures with a light heart.   He does not
need to prove his faith to any one.   He does not need to
stand up to a test or even to remain true to himself.   He
must needs wander, but there is no set purpose in his
journeyings.   His sufferings are as spiritual as corporeal.
He is aware too of the misery of others in the world.   And
in profound despair he must beg divine aid.

It is absurd to compare the plot of the whole novel with
the typical pattern of the Greek love romances and Fotis
with their heroines as Riefstahl does.[6]   The only great human love-story in Apuleius' main plot, that of Charite, is a
tragedy.   It is like the Greek Romances in being a story
of high life and in this too is unique among Apuleius'
novelle.   But it is utterly different from the Greek love
romances in structure and tone.   The only parallel to
them is to be found in the inset story of Cupid and Psyche.
Here the tale is of two young lovers unhappily separated
by the cruelty not of Fortune but of a greater goddess,
Venus herself.   And only after the hard testing of one of
the pair, this time the lady, are the two lovers reunited.
Thus the conventional happy ending of the plot is
achieved.   But for the author's philosophical mind such
a beautiful story must start with a touch of Platonic sym-
bolism in the very names of the lovers, Cupid and Psyche,
and must be concluded in high heaven, for only among
the immortals may such perfect happiness be won forever.

From this account of Apuleius' *Metamorphoses* it is already clear that his great novel is a synthesis of various
types of Greek Romances.   Its closest parallel is in the

---

6 Riefstahl, *op. cit.*, p. 85.

Greek *Lucius or Ass,* for the bare outline of the plot of the first ten books is like that of the Greek work. But all recent research tends to prove that Lucian's original *Metamorphoses* was satiric in character, therefore very different in tone from Apuleius' serious work. So although they share the characteristics of a romance of adventure, with stories of magic and of robbers forming principal episodes, the motivation and the aim of the two romances are utterly different. This difference is emphasized by Apuleius' two longest and most startling additions to the plot, the love-story of Cupid and Psyche and the story of Lucius and Isis.

Apuleius writes a love romance like the Greek only in the story of Cupid and Psyche. For the episode with Fotis is a sex-story of convenience and the Milesian Tales added to the plot of *Lucius or Ass* carry out this Fotis-motif of sex and lechery.[7] The one long love-story of human beings, Charite's story, is indeed a love romance of a noble lady and her noble lord, but it is a complete tragedy in episodes, tone and ending. Only the Cupid and Psyche story is the true type of Greek love romances.

The third great interest in the Greek Romances besides adventure and love was religion. To this Apuleius gave a new emphasis and a new importance. In the center of his novel in the inset story of Cupid and Psyche he pictures the old familiar Olympian gods in their conventional mythological characters, but as realistically and with as implicit a satire as Lucian used in his "Dialogues of the Gods." Venus is a very jealous and cruel step-mother. Jupiter is a lusty, amorous, irresistible king. Cupid is at first undutiful, mischievous and wanton. The story of Lucius and Isis is, however, a serious story of a great reli-

[7] For an account of Aristides and the Milesian Tales see L. C. Purser, *The Story of Cupid and Psyche as related by Apuleius,* London, 1910, Excursus I.

gious experience. Through prayer, visions, priestly instruction, ceremonials, initiation and communion Apuleius becomes one with the goddess to whom he is to devote the rest of his life. The worship of Isis is pictured spiritually from the depths of experience by Apuleius who according to his own statements had actually been many times initiated in her cult.[8]

Throughout these three parts of Apuleius' novel with their successive emphasis on adventure, love and religion, virtually all the conventional devices of the Greek Romances are employed. In the stories of adventure there are rapidly shifting scenes, though in a more limited spatial area. The Greek love romances lie according to the time of their action in the geography of the colonies of great Greece or within the boundaries of the hellenistic-oriental world from Byzantium to Egypt, from Sicily to Babylon. The action is carried out through long sea voyages, varied with storms and shipwreck. The wide world, the spatial separations are overcome only through the faithfulness of the lovers. The Ass-story takes place in narrower compass, in old Greece between Patrae, Hypata and Corinth. To Lucian's geographical set Apuleius adds Rome. In these two versions of the Ass-story all the life of mankind is represented concretely and in close perspective. The action concerns little people living in one locality or for purposes of trade taking short journeys hither and thither on land.[9] Other conventional devices in Apuleius' stories of adventure are the introduction as important characters of robbers and robber chieftains, narratives with emphasis on external events, descriptions like that of the robbers' cave.

In the love-story of Charite the interest centers in a lover and his lass ; both are persons in high life, both are faithful.

---

[8] *Apologia*, 55, 56.   [9] Riefstahl, *op. cit.*, pp. 84–85.

A dream furnishes an apparition of the dead husband. But the villainy of a treacherous friend makes the story a tragedy involving murder and suicide. The story of Cupid and Psyche, true to the type of the Greek love romance, starts with a religious beginning, the worship of a mortal girl Psyche as the goddess of love ; is motivated by a Greek oracle ; describes at length the proving of the heroine in tasks imposed by the will of an unfriendly deity ; depicts Psyche's apparent sleep of death ; and finally consummates a happy ending for the lovers through a saving god, who is Cupid the hero himself. A pastoral note which affiliates the story with *Daphnis and Chloe* is introduced by the presence of the friendly god Pan, who acts as a wise old adviser and comforter to Psyche in her great despair. And the conventional use of *excursus* creates a new pictorial character in brilliant descriptions of Venus charioted over the sea, of the Palace of Cupid, of Cupid asleep, of the wedding banquet of the lovers.

In the story of Lucius and Isis in Book Eleven, many of the conventional devices of the Greek Romances appear : dreams, epiphanies, religious festivals, a *dea ex machina*. So in Chariton Aphrodite and Fortune contend for the control of the lovers ; in Xenophon of Ephesus Artemis and Isis are the two saving goddesses ; in Heliodorus Apollo and Isis are prominent though the philosophies of the Gymnosophists and of the Neo-Pythagoreans have a share in the plot ; in Achilles Tatius Artemis reigns supreme ; in Longus Pan and the Nymphs guide the destinies of the young lovers. The difference in Apuleius is that the whole quest of the hero is for some meaning in life and when magic, adventure, mythology and human amours can not supply it, he finds through conversion a union with a mystic goddess who sublimates his emotion and absorbs his life into her service.

The greater subjectivity of the Apuleius' romance as compared to the Greek Romances is attained by the aloneness of the hero, his quest and its implicit meaning, his individual satisfaction. This subjectivity is intensified by the complete adoption of the ego-narrative. Far more attention is paid by Apuleius than by the Greek romancers to the narrator and to his point of view in telling the whole romance. Achilles Tatius was afterwards to attempt the use of this device of narration in the first person, but he soon lost sight of the narrator in the narrative and even at the end he never let him reappear. Lucian adopted completely the *ich-roman* form, but, as far as can be known, without rich characterization of the teller. Apuleius uses to the full the advantage of having a man-ass as narrator, for his composite hero has a duplex view-point of man and animal and displays a double humor, of man and beast. All this keeps the hero-narrator before our eyes and we become ever more and more interested in the effect of the events narrated on his inner life and on his final solution of life.

Riefstahl points out that in the Greek love romances there is some striving after subjectivity in the presentation of external events. The possibility of expression is not yet rich, but by soliloquies, by descriptions of emotions, by reflections on events expressed in γνῶμαι the romancers are working from objective to subjective presentation of their material. The soul is treated as an individual entity separated from the body and contrasted to it. On this foundation in the love romances rests the inner structural arch of spatial separation and spiritual fidelity. The relation of the objective and the subjective creates somehow the scale on which all these romances take their place. The love romances are at the objective end of the scale, the older ones particularly, dynamic events holding writer and reader spell-bound. In Longus a peaceful atmosphere is created because there are few exciting events, little travel, only the study of the development of love in two adolescents in a quiet pastoral setting, but the expression is not adequate. Longus senses the dual conception of Eros, in man and in nature, for the love of the two young shepherds is set in the teeming, growing life of the outer world, but he does not develop fully this subtle implication. Achilles Tatius inclines toward the subjective direction through his attempted use of the ego-narrative. But the fullest subjective treatment is found in Apuleius. In Achilles Tatius as in Apuleius, the aim of the hero is a μυστήριον but with him it is the μυστήριον of love ; in Apuleius it is the *sacrorum arcana*.[10] The powerful cosmic force of love appears only in Apuleius and there it is embodied in the personality of Isis. The goddess describes herself to Lucius as "the natural mother of all things, mistress and governess of all the elements, the initial progeny of worlds, chief of the powers divine, queen of all that are in hell, the principal of them that dwell in heaven, manifested above and under one form of all the gods and goddesses." [11]

The whole story of Apuleius pictures, according to Riefstahl, the striving of the individual towards the All. The cosmic Eros has taken the place of the ancient Greek Eros, who was a terrible power, often identified with the blind, cruel Τύχη. To this cosmic Eros Apuleius has given the name of Isis.[12] Riefstahl to be sure pushes too far his theory of an underlying philosophical content in Apuleius, representing the romance "as an artistic unit . . . and as an issue of the writer's intellectual interests and personality," "ein künstlerisch gestaltetes Anschauungsbild der

[10] *Met.* XI. 22.
[11] S. Gaselee, *Apuleius the Golden Ass being the Metamorphoses of Lucius Apuleius, in The Loeb Classical Library*, XI. 4.

[12] For Riefstahl's whole theory of "Apuleius und die griechischen Liebesromane" see *op. cit.*, pp. 82–95.

existenziellen Lebensgrundlage des Neuplatonismus." [13]
Yet he does point out astutely the fundamental difference
in Apuleius which makes his *Metamorphoses* another dis-
tinct type of romance, the subjective philosophical.

A word now in retrospect.   By the end of the second
century A.D., this new genre of literature, the romance, had
developed to full stature.   Already besides the author of
the Ninus romance, Chariton, Lucian and Apuleius had
written their stories, and perhaps also Xenophon of Ephesus.   The different types of romance were already established : the historical romance, the love romance with its
secondary interests of adventure and religion, satirical romance, the subjective philosophical romance.   The pastoral was soon to be added.   That is, in the second century
of our era, a new type of literature was created, a type
which was to be the most popular in the modern world.[14]

It is strange to find that so distinguished and perceptive
an historian as Rostovtzeff in his histories of Rome does
not recognize the significance for the early empire of this
new literary form.   In describing the second century, he
writes : [15]

"Except for the troubled reign of Marcus Aurelius, the Roman
Empire under the Antonines enjoyed profound peace, broken only
by distant wars on the frontier.   Within the empire life appeared
to be, as it had been in the first century, a steady forward movement
for the diffusion and enrichment of civilization.   The creative
power of Rome seemed to have reached its zenith.   There was,

[13] See the review of Riefstahl's
work by H. W. Prescott in *A.J.P.*, 61
(1940), pp. 115–17.

[14] To complete the list of different
types of novels, we might add the
realistic novel of low life, Petronius'
Satyricon. Since its affiliations are
with the Menippean satire and not
with the Greek Romances, I have
omitted any study of it here. See
E. H. Haight, *Apuleius and his Influence*, pp. 7–8; "Satire and the
Latin Novel" in *Essays on Ancient
Fiction*, pp. 86–120. For a recent
review of the literature about the
Satyricon and a brilliant re-interpre-
tation of it see Gilbert Highet "Petronius the Moralist" in *T.P.A.P.A.*,
LXXII (1941), 176–94.

[15] M. Rostovtzeff, *A History of the
Ancient World, Volume II. Rome*,
Oxford, 1927, pp. 239–41. Yet see pp.
181–85 for Rostovtzeff's knowledge of
the Greek Romances.

however, one disquieting symptom : after the brilliant age of the Flavians we note an almost complete sterility in literature and art. After Tacitus, and after the artists who worked for Trajan . . . the decades that followed failed to produce a single great writer or a single notable monument of art. . .

"Even before the time of war and pestilence in the reign of Marcus Aurelius, we mark in the whole of intellectual life not merely a pause but even a backward movement. The only exception is a revival of Greek rhetorical prose, perfect in form but monotonous in substance. Its chief representative is the sophist and rhetorician, Aristides, and his best work is his *Panegyric* on Rome. The *Dialogues* of Lucian are witty and interesting ; he was a sceptic and a humorist who mocked all ideals both new and old. In the West there are only two names to be quoted, that of the satirist Juvenal, a gloomy and bitter observer of the dark side of human life, and that of Pliny the Younger, a shallow orator and a brilliant representative of the epistolary style. The rest both in Greece and in Italy are writers of handbooks, text-books, and of miscellaneous collections of entertaining stories for the amusement and instruction of the reader."

Rostovtzeff's omission of all reference to the Greek Romances (even to Lucian's) and to Apuleius shows how completely they have been disregarded. Yet for a picture of the social life of the second and the third centuries and of the psychology of the men of the time the Greek Romances and Apuleius are a revelation.

The Roman empire had checked both political activity and oratory, indeed the orator had been succeeded by the rhetor in Greece and Rome. In the unified Mediterranean world trade had developed greatly and travellers had followed traders from one country to another, among them the lecturing sophists. The new lands visited had their curiosities and splendors so travellers' tales multiplied with descriptions often worthy of a natural history. Men, diverted from the aims of personal ambition which military conquest or a democratic state had afforded, now sought release and excitement in the personal relations. Women achieved a new freedom and a new importance. The emotional life came to have a new interest and this led to the development of the prose romance.

From the east came, with rich material resources, a wealth of new ideas, a mingling of superstition, magic, religion and philosophy. Just as man's emotions were turned inward so was his thought. The greatest new adventure became the quest for a solution of life itself. The romances of the early empire whatever their type reflect the age : its craving for excitement, its desire for adventure, its dread of brigands, its curiosity about the new, its interest in art, its wish for fulfillment of emotion in romantic love, its awareness of unsolved mysteries in man and the universe. With even the partial re-dating of the Greek Romances all sorts of subjects open up for investigation such as the apparatus of religion in the use of oracles, dreams, epiphanies ; the interest in works of art ; the new position of women. At any time in the future new fragments of romances may be discovered, or new dating of some of the old ones may be made possible. But even now while archaeological discoveries are suspended and publication of new editions is delayed, we may read and re-read these amazing old stories and see what escape literature was in the second and third centuries. The Greek Romances have much to tell us of the psychology of their authors, their characters, and their readers. They have a deep human value.

"Homo sum : humani nil a me alienum puto."

INDEX

A

Achilles, 11, 20, 35, 78, 90, 115, 173
Achilles Tatius, 10, 11, 12, 13, 62, 63, 95-118, 120, 196, 197, 198
Clitophon and Leucippe, 95-118, list of characters, 97-98
Aeschines, 147
Aesculapius, 155, 187
Aethiopica, 61-94
Africa, 186, 187
Alcinous, 79, 173
Alexander Romance, 11, 12
Alexandria, 45, 46, 47, 95, 99, 101, 117
Allinson, F. G., ix, 172, 175
Amyot, Jacques, 120, 143
Andromeda, 75, 93, 115
Antioch, 144
Antonius Diogenes, *The Wonderful Things beyond Thule*, 12, 145, 170, 171, 172
Apollonius of Tyre, 12
Apollonius of Tyana, 62, 88, 89
Apparent deaths, 100, 103-4, 196
Anthia, 12, 38-60, 93
Antinous, 92
Antoninus Pius, 187
Aphrodite, 8, 10, 16, 20, 21, 26, 28, 31, 32, 33, 51, 103, 107, 110, 196
Apis, 52, 55
Apollo, 42, 51, 55, 67, 68, 78, 82, 86, 87, 88, 111, 196
Apollonius Rhodius, 4
Apuleius, viii, 6, 13, 54, 145, 186-201
Metamorphoses, 176, 180, 181, 186-99
Cupid and Psyche, 186, 189, 191, 192, 193, 194, 196
Apologia, 187, 195
Florida, 187
Plato and his Doctrine, 187
The God of Socrates, 187
Aradus, 19, 20, 32, 35

Ares, 44, 51, 53, 183
Aristaenetus, 108
Aristides, author of *Milesian Tales*, 5, 194
Aristides, author of *Panegyric* on Rome, 200
Aristippus, 169
Aristophanes, 113, 149, 166, 167, 172
Aristotle, 153
Armenia, 156
Artemis, 40, 42, 51, 53, 103, 111, 112, 113, 196
Asia Minor, 14, 15, 53, 144
Astarte, 115
Athenagoras, 15
Athens, 77, 151, 153, 155, 186
Augustine, Saint, 187
Augustus, 40, 155
Aurelian, 62

B

Babylon, 10, 20, 26, 29, 32, 33, 34
Bardèche, Maurice, 59
Berytus, 98, 101
Bessa, 70, 77
Bias, 27
Bion, 135
Bithynia, 158
Blake, Warren E., viii, 14
Bonaparte, Elisa, 142
Bonaparte, Napoleon, 142
Borden, Fanny, ix
Bornecque, H., 6
Burton, William, 96
Byron, Lord G. G. N., 141
Byzanthium, 98, 101, 105, 195

C

Caldarini, Aristide, 4, 6, 13, 35, 36, 51, 54, 63, 76, 80, 88, 91, 95, 135, 136, 137